LORD,
TEACH US

The Lord's Prayer & the
Christian Life

WILLIAM H. WILLIMON
& STANLEY HAUERWAS
WITH SCOTT C. SAYE

ABINGDON PRESS
Nashville

LORD, TEACH US: THE LORD'S PRAYER & THE CHRISTIAN LIFE

This book is printed on recycled, acid-free paper.

Cataloguing in Publication data is available from the Library of Congress.

Scripture quotations unless otherwise labeled are from the New Revised Standard Version Bible, Copyright © 1989 by the Division of Christian Education of the National Council of the Churches of Christ in the USA. Used by permission.

The English translation of The Lord's Prayer on page 7 is by the International Consultation on English Texts, 1275 "K" Street NW, #1202, Washington, D.C. 20005-4097.

The Epigraph on page 9 is from Frederick Buechner, *Listening to Your Life* (San Francisco: HarperCollins). Copyright © 1992 by Frederick Buechner. Used by permission.

12 13 14 15 16 – 25 24 23 22 21 20 19

MANUFACTURED IN THE UNITED STATES OF AMERICA

To
Joanna Hauerwas
Mary Gilbert
Alberta Parker
Ruby Willimon
Mothers who taught us to pray

Our Father in heaven,
   hallowed be your name,
   your kingdom come,
   your will be done, on earth as in heaven.
Give us today our daily bread.
Forgive us our sins
   as we forgive those who sin against us.
Save us from the time of trial
   and deliver us from evil.
For the kingdom, the power, and the glory are yours
   now and for ever. Amen.

EPIGRAPH

In the Episcopal Order of Worship, the priest sometimes introduces the Lord's Prayer with the words, "Now, as our Savior Christ hath taught us, we are bold to say, . . . " The word bold is worth thinking about. We do well not to pray the prayer lightly. It takes guts to pray it at all. We can pray it in the unthinking and perfunctory way we usually do only by disregarding what we are saying.

"Thy will be done" is what we are saying. That is the climax of the first half of the prayer. We are asking God to be God. We are asking God to do not what we want but what God wants. We are asking God to make manifest the holiness that is now mostly hidden, to set free in all its terrible splendor the devastating power that is now mostly under restraint. "Thy kingdom come . . . on earth" is what we are saying. And if that were suddenly to happen, what then? What would stand and what would fall? Who would be welcomed in and who would be thrown the Hell out? Which if any of our most precious visions of what God is and of what human beings are would prove to be more or less on the mark and which would turn out to be phony as three-dollar bills? Boldness indeed. To speak those words is to invite the tiger out of the cage, to unleash a power that makes atomic power look like a warm breeze.

You need to be bold in another way to speak the second half. Give us. Forgive us. Don't test us. Deliver us. If it takes guts to face the omnipotence that is God's, it takes perhaps no less to face the impotence that is ours. We can do nothing without God. Without God we are nothing.

It is only the words "Our Father" that make the prayer bearable. If God is indeed something like a father, then as something like children maybe we can risk approaching him anyway.

—Frederick Buechner, Listening to Your Life

CONTENTS

INTRODUCTION

"Teach us to pray!"

Jesus' disciples asked him, "Show us the Father," or "Save me!" or "Lord, where are you going?" On one occasion, they asked, "Who among us will be the greatest?" Jesus did not always answer, probably because their questions were misstated. It is a great achievement to ask the right questions. So it is important that Jesus did teach them how to pray. The disciples had finally asked the right question.

This is a book for people who are becoming Christian, who are trying to learn to ask the right questions. Because of the nature of the Christian faith, all of us, no matter how long we have been around Jesus, are always learning anew how to ask the right questions. No one of us ever becomes so faithful, so bold in our discipleship, that we become experts in being Christian.

Think of Christianity, not primarily as a set of doctrines, a volunteer organization, or a list of appropriate behaviors. Think of Christianity as naming a journey of a people. As you read the Gospels, you will note that Jesus and his disciples are always on the way somewhere else, breathlessly on the move:

Then he went about among the villages teaching. He called the twelve and began to send them out two by two, and gave them

13

*authority . . . . He ordered them to take nothing for their journey
except a staff; no bread, no bag, no money.* (Mark 6:6b-8)

The journey is an adventure in ç reat part because it is a
trip with Jesus, a trip toward trust in him rather than trust in
those securities and crutches in which the world has taught
us to trust (i.e., bread, bags, and money).

By praying the Lord's Prayer we are being made into a
people whose journey is a sign to the world that God has not
abandoned the world to its own devices but is present as a
people on the move, a people moving out from their old ways
and means, ordinary people who have been given the extraordinary authority to be part of the divine assault upon
the realm of evil as those who *"cast out many demons, and
anointed with oil many who were sick and cured them"* (Mark
6:13).

The journey is dangerous. Martin Luther said that, when-
ever the work of Christ occurs, demons move into action. So,
in the passage from Mark that speaks of Jesus commissioning
his disciples to go out with him on a journey to cast out
demons and to heal the sick, Mark immediately says, *King
Herod heard of it* (Mark 6:14). By his mention of a politician's
name, King Herod, Mark reminds us that the journey with
Jesus is also a journey toward the cross. The principalities
and powers do not take kindly to a group of ordinary people
breaking loose, letting go of the world's securities, and moving out with Jesus.

Because the journey called Christianity is potentially dangerous, this is also a book about prayer, Christian prayer,
how to be a Christian by learning how to pray as a Christian.
There are many books that attempt to "explain" Christianity,
as if Christianity is a set of interesting ideas or a set of beliefs.
By affirming a minimal selection of these beliefs, Christianity
is supposed to give your life meaning and purpose, or fulfill
some set of expectations you had in mind before you met
Christianity.

14

We have nothing against your life being more meaningful, but that is not primarily what the Christian faith is about. Rather, to be a Christian is to have been drafted to be part of an adventure, a journey called God's kingdom. Being part of this adventure frees us from the terrors that would enslave our lives if we were not part of the journey.

Jesus was not a philosopher laying out a new system of disembodied belief. Jesus was a teacher whose life taught what he preached. We love and follow Jesus not simply because of what he said, but because of the way he lived, died, and was resurrected. Jesus did not ask us to agree with him but to follow him. He takes us on a journey, not just toward Jerusalem, but toward truth, toward a Kingdom we would not have entered without his saying, *"Follow me"* (Mark 1:17).

So *Lord, Teach Us* presents the Christian faith not as a set of beliefs but rather as a prayer that you must learn to pray. Along the way, we will discuss doctrines, but Christian doctrines are like prayer, a set of practices. The doctrines are meant to help us to pray, "Our Father. . . ." This book is shaped by the Lord's Prayer because the prayer is a mark of the journey called Christian. The prayer names the danger you will face as well as providing the help—the necessary skills—you will need for negotiating the dangers of the journey. Christianity means conflict. We never forget, as we pray, that the one who taught us to pray in this way was crucified.

We pray like this because, in Jesus of Nazareth, God has intruded among us in a spectacularly weird and peculiarly wonderful way. Like most wonderful things in our lives, God being with us creates an oddness—indeed we become odd as we respond to Jesus because, in the world's eyes, Jesus is odd. Don't pray this prayer if you don't want to be odd.

There are many people who know very little about the Christian faith but who already know the Lord's Prayer. We hope to demonstrate that, in praying in the Lord's Prayer, Christians keep being confronted by the oddness, the radicalness of learning to pray as Jesus taught.

Because God has come among us as Jesus, being a Christian is *not* something that comes naturally. It doesn't "make sense" in the ways we are taught to make sense. There are all kinds of prayer, but prayer as Jesus taught is a peculiar kind of activity based upon the life, death, and resurrection of Jesus. We don't decide to become Christians and then find that the Lord's Prayer is a helpful means of expressing our faith. We don't choose this prayer; it chooses us. It reaches out to us, forms us, invites us into the adventure called discipleship. Being Christian is a result of having been initiated (baptized) into a group of people (church) who are shaped by peculiar practices like Christian prayer.

We cannot convince you that Christianity is "true" prior to your learning to pray this prayer. If you come to the Christian faith with some theory about what it would take for the Christian faith to be "true," for instance, that it was "true to my experience of God" or "it seems reasonable to me," then you ought to worship your theory of truth—that your experience is God or that your reason is divine—rather than praying the Lord's Prayer.

Jesus told those who believed in him: *"If you continue in my word, you are truly my disciples; and you will know the truth, and the truth will make you free"* (John 8:31-32). He also said to them, *"I am the way, and the truth, and the life"* (John 14:6). Note that being formed as a disciple is prior to knowing the truth. As we submit ourselves to discipleship, we learn to be people who are truthful. Truth is not a set of propositions about the world; rather, truth is Jesus Christ. We know truth by coming to know this person and we know this person by learning to pray as he taught us.

Pray in This Way

To be a Christian is to submit one's life to trustworthy authorities who can teach us rightly to pray. Therefore, when Jesus' disciples asked him about prayer (Luke 11), Jesus told them to "pray in this way"—like some poor man who kept pestering his neighbor at midnight, beating on his door until he got out of bed and gave him the bread he needed (Luke 11:5-13). We ought to be similarly persistent in our effort to "pray in this way." In the process of obeying Jesus' command to pray like this, our lives are bent toward God in a way that is not of our natural inclination and we become as we pray, namely Christian.

Because this submission, this bending of our lives toward God does not come naturally, we ask you to memorize this prayer, to repeat it again and again. Repetition reminds us that this prayer was not our idea. In committing it to memory, we commit it to heart, for as we shall see the Christian heart is constituted by memory.

Because the world can be a dangerous place for Christians, because the world is always assaulting us with other accounts of reality, always offering up other prayers to other gods, memorizing this prayer is an essential skill for survival as a Christian. Even this prayer can be prayed falsely. We shall see how it makes all the difference that we learn to pray among skillful practitioners.

Thus the usual place to say this prayer is on Sunday, in church, amid the Body of Christ. Joining our voices with others in the repetition of this prayer, we are reminded that being a Christian is too tough to go alone. This is public theology. We admit that we would never have known how to pray as a Christian had not the church reached out to us through baptism and taught us this prayer. Sometimes you will want to reject God's incorporation into the body called the church. Don't feel guilty for getting fed up with the church. Church is not easy. Yet it is our claim that living into your baptism and learning to pray in public, in the body, will make you truly happy.

The church traditionally instructed new Christians by teaching them this prayer. We want to teach you the best that we know. At least that helps to identify who we are.

So if you are asked, "Who is a Christian?" the best answer you can give is, "A Christian is none other than someone who has learned to pray the Lord's Prayer."

Learning to pray this prayer, allowing it to become second nature to us, takes time, habit. We pray out of habit. Sometimes people say, "I often feel guilty that, when I'm praying the Lord's Prayer, I'm not really thinking about what I'm praying. I just say the words out of habit." Habit is good. Most of the really important things we do in life, we do out of habit. We eat, sleep, make love, shake hands, hug our children out of habit. Some things in life are too important to be left up to chance. Some things in life are too difficult to be left up to spontaneous desire—things like telling people that we love them or praying to God. So we do them "out of habit." Thus, in the church we generally do the same things over and over again, week after week, telling the same stories and singing the same songs.

Some complain that this makes church boring. While we do not defend boredom (for it is a sin against the joyful adventure of following Jesus), we do say that habits are important, particularly in a faith that is so against our natural inclinations, a faith that is so at odds with many of the deeply ingrained and widely held assumptions of this culture. We therefore must do things "out of habit" as Christians because it is so difficult for us to pay attention to God in a society that offers us so many distractions. As we have said, prayer is bending our lives toward God. Habit is one way we do that.

When the disciples asked Jesus about prayer, he did not tell them to go off and sit quietly until something spiritual came to their minds. He did not ask them, "Well, how do you feel about God?" He said, "Pray like this. 'Our Father . . . .'"

This prayer is a gift. One of the most difficult aspects of meeting new people is not knowing what to say at first. How should we address them? What subject should we bring up first? In giving us this prayer, Jesus has not left us to our own devices in our relationship to God. We need not flail around, trying to think up something to say to God. All we have to do is to say these words out of habit, by heart.

It is the *Lord's* prayer. We, who are accustomed to thinking of prayer as a good strategy for getting what we want ("The family who prays together stays together") and an appropriate opening for football games and important civic meetings, may be surprised that we must be taught to pray. This prayer is not for getting what we want but rather for bending our wants toward what God wants. This is the Lord's Prayer, prayer "in Jesus' name," which means that this prayer, unlike some other modes of prayer, is distinctively related to the one who teaches us to pray. This prayer is the enactment of the story of a God who called a people into existence through Jesus. In praying this prayer we become the people God has called us to be in Jesus.

The notion of the necessity of being taught to pray may sound odd. It is supposed to sound odd in a society that worships individual autonomy, freedom, and detachment, a culture that has taught us to live so that we are determined by no tradition, that we are accountable to nothing outside the self. In such a culture, we get confused into thinking that it is possible to pray by ourselves, on our own.

Because it is possible to pray falsely, we never pray "by ourselves." Someone is always teaching us, forming us. We may be "taught" by a capitalist economy, rather than the Christian faith, but we will be taught. Most of us have been taught that religion is something we ought to choose for ourselves. We don't remember being taught this because choosing for ourselves is a value so widely held in this society, so firmly sanctioned by the economic order and the government, that choosing for ourselves seems natural, innate. In so believing we demonstrate how well a consumer society has formed us, turning our lives into a mere matter of consumer preference without our even remembering when we were taught. We did not choose to believe that personal choice is the highest human virtue. Rather, we were taught, formed, forced to believe that nothing is important in life other than that which we have personally chosen. The irony is that the belief that nothing is important in life other than that which we have personally chosen is a belief that we have not personally chosen! The supermarket and shopping mall have been our school.

The schools teach us that all choices are more or less equal. Thus we believe we should never tell anyone what they should or should not choose. After all, we are told, all choices are equal. Accordingly all religions must also be equal. You simply choose the one that best suits your lifestyle.

Yet to learn to pray Jesus' prayer means we believe we are being made righteous, worthy members of God's kingdom. Does this mean that Christians believe that we are "better" than other people? Interestingly, in the Gospel of Matthew, the Lord's Prayer occurs in a section of that Gospel in which Jesus is attacking religious self-righteousness among his own followers:

"When you are praying, do not heap up empty phrases as the Gentiles do; for they think that they will be heard because of their many words. Do not be like them, for your Father knows what you need before you ask him.

"Pray then this way: . . . ." (Matthew 6:7-9)

By learning to pray the Lord's Prayer, we do not become better than other people—at least in the sense that "better" is used in our society. We do not become better; we become Christian. That is, we become disciples of Jesus who have no need to claim that we are better than other people since our

20

prayer now is a witness to what God has done among ordinary sinful folk like us by teaching us how to pray.

In praying as Jesus taught us, does this mean that there is something wrong with the prayer of a Buddhist or a Hindu? The very question shows that we may not have yet learned to pray in Jesus' name. The prayer of a Buddhist or a Hindu is distinct from the prayer of a Christian and ought to be respected for its distinctiveness. In Christian prayer, we ask not to be considered better but rather that we be allowed to pray and thus to witness to the God who has made even people like us truthful worshipers through Jesus Christ our Lord.

If we are Christian, if we have learned to pray "in Jesus' name," it is God's doing rather than our doing. Remember: this is the Lord's prayer. We didn't think of it. So when someone asks about Buddhist or Hindus or ordinary modern American secular people and whether or not they will be "saved," it shows a misunderstanding of being "saved." Salvation, Christian salvation, is not some individual relationship between me and God. Rather, salvation is being drafted into an adventure, having our lives commandeered by God to go on a journey called the Christian faith. This prayer, this "Our Father," is the naming of, and the participation in, the means whereby we are saved. This is the way God makes us part of a kingdom through which we are saved from the world.

What God does for Buddhists and Hindus is God's business. All we do in the Lord's Prayer is to testify to God, and anyone else who will listen, how God has dealt with us. Being saved is not some individual achievement, not the result of some flash of personal insight, nor the securing of life's sense of meaning, although all of that may happen in the process of praying this prayer. Salvation is the delightful surprise of having your little life caught up in the purposes of God for the whole world. Salvation is having your life bent toward God when all you thought you were doing was memorizing a little prayer. Salvation is having the courage to tell the world what has happened to you now that God in Christ has intruded among us.

The Lord's Prayer is a lifelong act of bending our lives toward God in the way that God has offered—"thy will be done, thy kingdom come." We have quite enough teaching in the various modes of achieving our will in this world. We build our kingdoms all over the world and the wreckage is all around us.

Do you find it curious that we talk about "bending" rather than "believing"? Perhaps you thought this was going to be a book on "Major Christian Beliefs," an enumeration of various important Christian doctrines for you to think about. Isn't Christianity about believing in Christian doctrines?

No. Not because doctrines are unimportant, but rather doctrines, propositions about the Christian faith—like "God is love" or "God is Father, Son, and Holy Spirit"—are derivative of the practices of Christianity—practices like worship, prayer, how we have sex, and what we do with our money. Doctrines and beliefs are efforts to remind us why it is important that we pray and how. The function of doctrine is to make Christian prayer as difficult as it ought to be.

While this book has been a joy to write, it has also been difficult. This is the third book we have done together. What to say to those who are "considering Christianity"? We developed a text but were unhappy with it. We thought our imaginations needed a kick. We found that kick in the person of Scott Saye. Scott is a graduate student in religion here at Duke. His contributions were so important that we felt that we should acknowledge his work by indicating "with Scott Saye" on the title page. Scott's insights greatly strengthened this book.

There are those who identify us as unrelenting critics of the church, a designation we have no doubt earned. Yet nothing is more important to us than for the church to live by the courage of its convictions. We hope this little book

22

will, in a modest way, help us all, beginners as well as lifelong Christians, so to live.

You might want to read one of the book's ten chapters each week, continuing to pray and reflect as you read. Although you may read the book alone, to find out more about the Christian faith, or to grow deeper in your faith in Christ, we think that the book will be best if shared with others who are on the journey with Christ with you.

So we ask you to begin by praying the Lord's Prayer. This is the fount from which all Christian belief and action flows, the daily bending of our lives toward a God who has, in Jesus Christ, so graciously leaned toward us.

William H. Willimon
Stanley M. Hauerwas

CHAPTER ONE

"Our Father"

Some people are offended that we are taught to address God as Father. The greater offense may be the little word *Our*. In this prayer we are taught to pray, not as individuals, but as the church.

When we say "Our," we are not being possessive. This God will not be our property. Many a person has come to grief attempting to domesticate God as a cheerleader for the American way or as a cosmic Federal Express. We say "Our" because of the astounding recognition that this God, the one who created the universe and flung the planets into their courses, the great God of heaven and earth, has willed to become our God. Before we reached out to God, God reached out to us and claimed us, promised to be our God, promised to make us God's people. Thus, not because of who we are or what we have done, but rather because of what God in Jesus Christ has done, we are privileged to say, "Our Father."

Thomas Aquinas says that we are created for no greater purpose than friendship with God. The "Our" reminds us that we cannot pray without friends. The habits that the prayer forms can be acquired only through friendship with others that makes possible our friendship with God. This is why you know a Christian by knowing who his or her friends are. But this does not mean that our friends are always the upright and the righteous. After all, Jesus was criticized for who he hung out with, *"a glutton and a drunkard, a friend of tax collectors and sinners"* (Matthew 11:19).

Jesus also called his disciples "friends":

"No one has greater love than this, to lay down one's life for one's friends. You are my friends if you do what I command you. I do not call you servants any longer, because the servant does not know what the master is doing; but I have called you friends, because I have made known to you everything that I have heard from my Father. You did not choose me but I chose you. And I appointed you to go and bear fruit." (John 15:3-16)

This passage from John's Gospel tells us much about our friendship with Jesus. Jesus is the friend who enacts friendship by laying down his life for his friends. As he is obedient to the will of his Father, daring to die for this motley crew he calls friends, so we are to be obedient to him as his friends. Yet we are not friends as equals. He says, "I do not call you servants any longer." Servants are those who can't figure out what the Master is doing. But here, the Master has transformed us from mere servants—those who merely obey the Master's will without knowing what the Master is up to— into friends by the Master's gracious willingness to reveal himself to us. What the Father has told the Son, the Son has made known to us servants, thus transforming us into friends.

After having called us "friends," Jesus gently reminds us that, "You did not choose me. I chose you." Our relationship to God—that we can boldly come to God saying "Our Father"—is due to God's choice of us, rather than our choice of God. God's choice of us is a gift that we often speak of in the church as "grace"—amazing grace. It's amazing particularly in a culture in which we are taught to believe that anything important is earned, achieved, worked for. Yet faith in Jesus as Lord can only come as a gift. To be a Christian is therefore to be the beneficiary of a two thousand year inheritance called "tradition," which none of us paid for, earned, much less deserved. Baptism reminds us that all of us have been adopted. We call it grace.

> *Once you were not a people,*
> *but now you are God's people.* (1 Peter 2:10)

Therefore it is never quite right to say things like, "Since *I* took Jesus into *my* heart," or "Since *I* gave my life to Christ." Our relationship to Jesus is his idea before it is ours. We don't take Jesus anywhere. He takes us places. Those who speak of having "a personal relationship with Christ," are right, it is personal. But it is not private. We are all in this together. Therefore, you will note that we say the Lord's Prayer out loud, thus demonstrating the public nature of this faith.

There is great comfort here. It is comforting to know that even though you don't always *feel* like a Christian, though you do not always *act* like a Christian, much less *believe* like a Christian, your relationship as friend of God is not based on what you have felt, done, or believed. Rather, you are friend with God because of God's choice of you in Jesus through the church. You are a Christian because you pray these words out loud, in public, out of habit, whether you feel like you want to pray at that moment or not. So Christians need not anxiously scan our inner thoughts, relentlessly examine our every deed and misdeed, close our eyes and earnestly attempt to believe ten absurd propositions before lunch. We can relax, safe in the knowledge that this whole thing between us and God was God's idea before it was ours. The journey with God is not a test to see if we can make the grade with God and be good enough to be friends with God. The journey begins with God in Christ calling us friends, inviting us to go because God wants us to be part of the

27

journey. Friendship with God is the name of the journey rather than its destination.

That's one reason why we persist in baptizing babies—helpless, dependent, sinful, little things that babies are—because each of us, at any age, is helpless, dependent, in need of God doing for us what we cannot do for ourselves.

That's one reason why we ask you to hold out your empty hands at the Eucharist (Lord's Supper) so as to demonstrate in a visible, physical way your hunger, your emptiness, and your need for God and God's people to give us our daily bread.

There's more to this little word "our" even than this. We not only joyfully declare that God is *"Our* Father," our friend and creator, but we say *"Our* Father," praying in the plural. Christian salvation would have been quite a different matter, if God had taught us to pray, "My Father, . . . give me this day my daily bread and lead me not into temptation . . . ."

There may be religions that come to you through quiet walks in the woods, or by sitting quietly in the library with a book, or rummaging around in the recesses of your psyche. Christianity is not one of them. Christianity is inherently communal, a matter of life in the Body, the church. Jesus did not call isolated individuals to follow him. He called a group of disciples. He gathered a crowd. (See Acts 2.)

Think how you got called to be a disciple. Is this something you thought of yourself? Was it revealed to you by staring up into the sun, or walking in a field of clover? No. You are here because of friendship with other Christians. Someone had to tell you the story. Someone had to live this faith in such a way that you said to yourself, "I want to know more about this. I want to be part of that." Somebody had to walk the walk and talk the talk. Perhaps it was a believing parent, of someone you met at work or in school, or by reading the Bible. This communal call was not accidental but integral to the Christian life. We get by only with help from our friends. Every time you say, "Our Father," you are naming the way we are saved—as a group, praying together, correcting one another, forgiving one another, stumbling along after Jesus together, memorizing the moves until his way has become our way. Our way.

As Christians we believe that our friends in faith extend not only to those who happen to be walking about at the present moment, but also those whom we call "the communion of the saints," that is, that great community of those who have gone before us in this faith. You are never alone in church. Every time we gather to pray, the saints pray with us, as if leaning down from the ramparts of heaven to join their voices with ours in the praise of God, as if to cheer us on in our current struggles to be faithful.

This means that you never have to pray on your own. Christian prayer is not like elementary school when the teacher would not allow you to look on someone else's paper during the quiz. The saints help us to pray. So, when pondering our relationship with God, we remember Aquinas and his words on friendship. Or we recall Martin Luther saying to his students, "I wish I could get you to pray the way my dog goes after meat!"

The church is therefore not just the grinning folk who greet you at the door on Sunday morning at St. John's on the Expressway, but also the saints from every age and place who lead you in prayer, who give you the words when you can't think of any, who reassure you that the journey with Jesus is worth walking, a journey that leads home.

We say, "Our Father." In calling God Father we are speaking first and foremost about Jesus' relationship to God, not our own. That is to say, God is called Father because we have come to know Jesus as the Son. "Father" and "Son" is the way we have been taught to name a certain relationship within the inner life of God. The important thing is not that these two terms are of the male gender, for Christians have always believed that God is greater than any human conceptions of gender. What is important is that these names attempt to describe the familial relationship that is part of God's own life. We can't say "Father" without remembering the Son; we can never know the Father unless the Son reveals the Father to us.

Of course, we all need fathers. Yet when Christians pray, "Our Father," we are not merely declaring that God created us. We are saying that, in Jesus Christ, God has saved us. Some people say they have difficulty believing in Jesus, but that they gladly believe in God on the basis of the evidence of God they see in nature. They look at the snowflake or the robin and, from what they think they see in creation, move to some vague awareness that there must be a Creator, some "Father," who created us and the world.

When Christians pray, "Our Father," we are not merely declaring that God created us. We are saying that, in Jesus Christ, God has saved us. That is, in praying, "Our Father," we are not looking at creation in order to deduce a creator, rather we are looking at the Son in order to know the Father. We're not saying something about the origin of creation but rather we are naming the nature of our salvation. Only because Jesus is the Son, do we know God as "Our Father."

Our relationship to God as Father finds expression in what is known as the Apostles' Creed: I believe in God the Father Almighty, maker of heaven and earth and in Jesus Christ his only Son, our Lord . . . .

Note that the creed assumes that we know God as Father prior to our knowledge of God as "maker of heaven and earth." So our knowledge of God begins, not with long walks in the woods, pondering the beauty of snowflakes, or meditating upon the stars. Our knowledge begins in no generalized, natural way. Rather, we know God only because God has been revealed to us by Jesus Christ. From our knowledge of God as Father, we are moved to a new understanding of what is going on in "heaven and earth," in snowflakes, the woods, and the stars. The one who has been revealed to us by Jesus as "Our Father" is also Creator.

God is not some great basket we can fill with any warm, fuzzy thoughts we choose; some amorphous something that is the mystery left over after we have explained everything else in life by other means.

God has a face, a name, a way of action: the Trinity. If we had not known Jesus, we would not have known God. If Jesus had not made us friends, we would not have known the depth of our enmity with God, all the ways we rebelled against God. We would not have known God; we would not have been in relationship with God. We would have gone our merry way assembling various false gods, quite content to name God as sex, or Mars, or money, or self-esteem, or whatever we happened to be in the market for at the moment.

Christians do not believe in the Trinity—God as Father, Son and Holy Spirit—because we have had certain experiences with God for which the Trinity is a helpful metaphor. Rather, in being taught to pray, "Our Father" we are taught to name God as Father, Son, and Holy Spirit. Jesus can teach us the name for God because Jesus is the Son.

In Galatians 4:6-7 we are told: *And because you are children, God has sent the Spirit of his Son into our hearts, crying, "Abba! Father!" So you are no longer a slave but a child, and if a child then also an heir, through God.* We therefore address God as "Father" metaphorically to refer to our relationship to God, a relationship that may also be explored with other metaphors like "mother" or "friend."

When we speak of God as "Father," we are not talking about the way each of us has a biological father. Rather we are saying that, through Christ, all biological fatherhood is relativized by our lifelong learning that God alone is our true Father. We do not call God "Father" because we have had certain positive experiences with our biological fathers and therefore project those experiences upon God. Rather all human fathers are measured, judged, and fall short on the basis of our experiences of God as Father. God the Father stands as judge against all human fatherhood. To pray to God

31

as the Father challenges the status quo of human fatherhood even as to call the church our family challenges the limitations and sins of the human family.

So when we pray, "Our Father," we are in a decisive way challenging the status of the family as it is known in our culture. For those who learn to pray like this, our first family is not our biological family but those who have taught us to pray, "Our Father." So Jesus said, "Call no one your father on earth, for you have one Father—the one in heaven" (Matthew 23:9). God is the Father. Family is the church. Christianity teaches us to look beyond our families and see our membership, through baptism, in *the* family that has been evoked from all families, nations, races, and cultures—the church. That's why you can gather in church with folk who ought—by the world's standards—to be perfect strangers to you and yet you call them "sister," "brother."

Thus the Trinity is integral to the way Christians live because the Trinity clearly indicates that God is a relation. Now we see why Jesus quite naturally wants to make us friends, for that is the way God is. God is a relationship, a friendship between Father, Son, and Holy Spirit. Naming God as Trinity is a way of declaring that the whole world was created to be in relationship. Trinity—God as Father, Son, and Holy Spirit—is a constant reminder to us that the whole world is being moved toward friendship, relationship, that nothing, no beetle or bullfinch, no believer or nonbeliever exists in isolation from the trinitarian God who is always moving everything toward relationship with God. The God who created us is the God who came to us as Jesus of Nazareth who is forever seeking us as Holy Spirit. We pray "Our Father," because we have been enticed by the infinitely resourceful Trinity toward a God who has made us restless until our lives rest in him (Romans 8:25).

Even when we don't know how to pray, don't know what to say to God, the Trinity helps us. Paul says none of us really knows what to say to God. Fortunately, the Holy Spirit helps us speak:

The Spirit helps us in our weakness; for we do not know how to pray as we ought, but that very Spirit intercedes with sighs too deep for words. And God, who searches the heart, knows what is the mind of the Spirit, because the Spirit intercedes for the saints according to the will of God. (Romans 8:26-27)

We do not know how to pray as Christians. When it comes down to it, what do we know of how to live, act, believe, and feel as Christians? Fortunately for us, what we know is not the point. The point is that, as Father, Son, and Holy Spirit, God has searched us and known us, has helped us in our weakness, has interceded for us even when we thought we were interceding for ourselves.

Therefore we are bold to say, "Our Father. . . ."

CHAPTER TWO

"In heaven"

You have not come to something that can be touched, a blazing fire, and darkness, and gloom, and a tempest, and the sound of a trumpet, and a voice whose words made the hearers beg that not another word be spoken to them. . . . for indeed our God is a consuming fire. (Hebrews 12:18-19, 29)

That we pray to God in heaven is a reminder that we become part of a large struggle by praying this prayer. This thing between us and Jesus is not merely personal; it's cosmic. The God whom we have been taught by Jesus to address as "Our Father" is the one who rules the whole cosmos, who speaks in earthquake, wind, and fire. Any less of a god wouldn't do us much good. The good that needs doing in this world—good for the poorest of the poor, the sickest of the sick, the most desperate of the desperate—tends to be considerably larger than our mere social activism, charity, or politics. Things are cosmically out of hand. Evil is not just the nasty little things we do to one another. It's as if evil is organized, massive, subtle, deep, cosmic.

For our struggle is not against enemies of blood and flesh, but against the rulers, against the authorities, against the cosmic powers of this present darkness, against the spiritual forces of evil in the heavenly places. (Ephesians 6:12)

If Jesus is no more than a helpful moral example, a wise teacher of ethics, an empathetic friend, then why pray at all? What good can even the best moral exemplar do for our ensnarement? After even our best moral efforts, after all our good deeds are done, there is still a great surplus of suffering and pain left over, still too much untouched evil. Therefore it makes a great deal of difference whether or not God hears us and acts when we pray. Otherwise our prayer is merely autosuggestion, self-therapy, not up to the battle.

It also makes a great deal of difference where God is when we pray. If Jesus resides safely tucked in our hearts, if God is only a wish projection of the very best of human aspiration and experience, then forget it. These little gods are no match for our big problems.

However, because we call God the Father who is "in heaven," we are bold to pray for such absurdly extravagant gifts as bread for the world, peace among the nations, healed marriages, cured cancer, rain. We are bold to pray for such gifts because we pray to the Father in heaven, the one who rules.

Our God is placed, located, has an address—heaven. This is not just a way of saying that God must be everywhere or God is nowhere. On the contrary our God is not everywhere, but somewhere. We have names for those places—the promise to Abraham on a starry night, the covenant with Israel, the law given to Moses, the land of Israel, the calling of King David, the prophets, the Temple, Jesus of Nazareth, the apostles, baptism, the Eucharist. God can be located in such places because our God is Lord of all God has made. Heaven is the name given to God's realm.

Our kingdoms are constantly being threatened by God's kingdom. Heaven is breaking out all over. God's realm intrudes into real places like Bethlehem, disrupting the lives of real people like Mary and Joseph, Caesar and Quirinius:

In those days a decree went out from Emperor Augustus that all the world should be registered. This was the first registration and was taken while Quirinius was governor of Syria. All went to their own towns to be registered. Joseph also went from the town of Nazareth in Galilee to Judea, to the city of David called Bethlehem, because he was descended from the house and family of David. He went to be registered with Mary, to whom he was engaged and who was expecting a child. (Luke 2:1-5)

Thus when the Creed speaks of Jesus as "seated at the right hand of God the Father Almighty," it is claiming that Jesus shares this rule with God. There is nothing that we go through here on earth that Jesus has not also endured. No petition we lay before the throne of God is more than the prayers Jesus prayed at Gethsemane and elsewhere. There, seated next to the right hand of God the Father Almighty, Jesus is able to intercede for us, as he prayed for his disciples. The Risen Christ is able to say, "What she is really trying to tell you is . . . . " Or, "What they wish they had the imagination to ask is . . . . "

It may seem odd to you that "Our Father" is located, by the prayer, "in heaven." Most of us think of ourselves as persons who want to get close to God. That is the god for whom we grope, if we grope for a god at all, a god to whom we can "get close," "a friend in need." This need to make God over into our own image has led some folk to speak of the need to develop "user-friendly churches." These churches are meant to be so much like the surrounding culture—churches fitted with padded pews whose sanctuaries resemble carpeted bedrooms with basketball gyms attached—that there we are never bumped by anything odd, never challenged by something weird.

Heaven is weird.

Just to pray to a God who is "in heaven," is a warning against contemporary domestication of God. Here is God who is not some pale image of ourselves and our best aspirations. This God doesn't live here in our country, is not housed within our sanctuaries. God the Father rules from heaven. So don't be confused by some Christian talk about "a personal relationship with Jesus," as if this were the whole point of the Christian faith—to get cozy and comfy with God. The God whom we address with the intimate, "Father" is also "in heaven." The God revealed in the Jew from Nazareth, Jesus, is the God who moves the sun and the stars.

Since, then, we have a great high priest who has passed through the heavens, Jesus, the Son of God, let us hold fast to our confession. For we do not have a high priest who is unable to sympathize with our weaknesses, but we have one who in every respect has been tested as we are, yet without sin. Let us therefore approach the throne of grace with boldness, so that we may receive mercy and find grace to help in time of need. (Hebrews 4:14-16)

Because God the Father and the Son reigns for ever and ever in heaven above and earth beneath, life is not just one thing after another, or even one blessed bit of luck after another. Life is lived under the providence of a loving, active, intruding God. In Jesus, we see that God the Father has a watchful eye. (God even notes when a sparrow bites the dust—Matthew 6:26.) God also has an open hand. (If we knock, the door will be opened—Matthew 7:7-8.) We know God the Father because God has been made known to us through the only Son. Now, God knows us through the revelation of the Son who, seated at the right hand of the Father in heaven, talks to the Father on our behalf.

Jesus the pioneer and perfecter of our faith, who for the sake of the joy that was set before him endured the cross, disregarding its shame, and has taken his seat at the right hand of the throne of God. (Hebrews 12:2)

37

Of course, some will say heaven is not a place. Heaven is an idea, a metaphor, a state of mind. No. When the Lord's Prayer speaks of God, it locates God. God is not some mushy, generalized pantheistic presence always and everywhere, therefore not now and nowhere. God is placed, enfleshed, incarnated through the people of Israel and in the person of Jesus of Nazareth. The God who is thus located is not some ephemeral presence who may have set the whole thing in motion and then slips into eternal elusiveness. Paul says that the same Spirit who teaches each of us to cry out, "Abba! Father!" is much more than merely personal—this is the cry of the whole cosmos itself.

We know that the whole creation has been groaning in labor pains until now; and not only the creation, but we ourselves, who have the first fruits of the Spirit, groan inwardly while we wait for adoption, the redemption of our bodies. (Romans 8:22-23)

Thus to say that God is in heaven is also to acknowledge that God can be as close to us as our own desires. After all, we are God's creatures. Just as an artist can continue to work with a piece of sculpture after it receives its initial form, so God continues to work through creation because it is God's creation. All creation longs to praise God, including heaven. In the Apostles' Creed we say, "I believe in God the Father, Almighty, creator of heaven and earth."

When I look at your heavens,
the work of your fingers,
the moon and the stars that
you have established; . . .
O LORD, our Sovereign,
how majestic is your name in
all the earth!
(Psalm 8:3, 9)

God chooses to be located within, not aloof from, God's created order in the person of Jesus. The person who purports to find God in every rock, tree, and glade is too often a pantheist who assumes that God is everywhere the same. But if God is everywhere, God is finally nowhere, and the world is empty. Christianity is really much more immanent (God is very close) than pantheism because our God promises to be in real places—Jerusalem—and actual faces—Jesus.

Furthermore, in heaven, God has a good view of us, all of us. When we look at things, our vision tends to be myopic. Most of the time it is difficult for us to see much beyond ourselves. God tends to take a larger view. Looking at the world, God's view is not limited by our national boundaries. Heaven provides a good vantage point for the whole picture:

> The LORD looks down from heaven;
> he sees all humankind.
> From where he sits enthroned he watches
> all the inhabitants of the earth.
> (Psalm 33:13-14)

Yet because our God is "in heaven," our God continues to stand at some distance from creation, for God is Creator, not created. God stands over against us in order to stand with us. This is not a fully appropriate analogy but try it on anyway: Every parent knows that, in order to be a good parent, you must not only be very close to your children—listening to them, spending time with them, talking to them—you must also be at some distance from your children—disciplining them, advising them, reminding yourself that your children are not mere extensions of you. God manages to do that with us. In heaven, God is intimately part of God's creation and its creatures at the same time God is not identical with creation.

We noted earlier that when we pray, we never pray alone. We always begin with "Our Father . . . ." Then we spoke of

39

"our" as the church present with you in prayer and noted that Christianity tends to be a group thing. Now, with the mention of heaven, we expand our notion of "our" so as to include all the saints, those who have died in the faith and who now enjoy God forever in heaven.

We are surrounded by so great a cloud of witnesses (Hebrews 12:1).

Heaven, according to the vision in the Revelation, is a crowded, raucous place, somewhat similar to St. Peter's Square in Rome on Easter or Glide Memorial in San Francisco on an average Sunday. Not only are there heavenly creatures—angels and others *numbered myriads of myriads and thousands of thousands*, which has to be a rather large number (Revelation 5:11)—but there are also the saints, those who have died in the faith and now rejoice full time in heaven.

> *"They are before the throne of God,*
> *and worship him day and night within his temple,*
> *and the one who is seated on the throne will shelter them.*
> *They will hunger no more, and thirst no more;*
> *the sun will not strike them,*
> *nor any scorching heat;*
> *for the Lamb at the center of the throne will be their shepherd,*
> *and he will guide them to springs of the water of life,*
> *and God will wipe away every tear from their eyes."*
> (Revelation 7:15-17)

So when we pray to the Father who is in heaven, we join our voices in a raucous, reverent chorus of prayer and praise. We call this "the communion of saints." At the Eucharist our banquet table extends all the way from our congregation to that great congregation made possible by Jesus' resurrection.

You may not be good with words. Don't worry. George Herbert, St. Francis, and Teresa of Avila pray with you. You may not have your head straight on Christian doctrine. Go ahead and pray with confidence. Thomas Aquinas, Martin Luther, and Georgia Harkness pray with you. You may find it difficult to make time to pray. Pray as often as you can. Your prayer joins those already in progress by Dietrich Bonhoeffer and Dorothy Day.

Our Christian hope is that, if we get good enough at participating in God's reign now, here on earth, we shall be ready fully to participate in God's final triumph eternally. We shall dwell forever in the house of the Lord (Psalm 23), a dwelling we have prepared for in our prayer here on earth.

CHAPTER THREE

"Hallowed be
your name"

God has a name. Modern people are sometimes tempted to think of God as a concept to which Christians have attached the label, "Father, Son, and Holy Spirit." They imagine God to be the sum of the highest and best aspirations of humanity, or a primitive way of thinking about morality, or the expression of that experience that each of us has when we are alone with our thoughts. But when we pray the Lord's Prayer, we say something different. We say that God is personal, God lives and acts, God has a name.

Back at the beginning of the Hebrew Exodus out of Egyptian slavery, God appears to Moses in the burning bush. Moses asks, "Who are you? Who am I supposed to say has sent me when I return to the Israelites?"

Moses realizes that he is not in the presence of a concept, some amorphous blob of spirit. He is face-to-face with a peculiar God who has peculiar ways of doing things. This God has heard the cry of an oppressed people. This God has not only heard but has been moved to act. This God is bigger than kings like Pharaoh. This God chooses strange, inept people like Moses to help disrupt things at the palace. What are you? Moses asks. Are you a concept like "liberation," or "self-esteem," or "freedom"? God's first answer is a puzzling conversation stopper: "I am who I am," or "I will be present to whom I am present." This God creates this God's own identity. Living, true, this God is not to be jerked about by every human whim and cry. This God is sovereign, free, untamed, compassionate, and holy.

Upon hearing God's name, Moses *hid his face, for he was afraid to look at God* (Exodus 3:6). And who wouldn't? To discover that God's ways or not our ways (Isaiah 55:8), that our God is not the patron of Pharaoh, not safely sealed in heaven but busy disrupting arrangements here on earth, is to be moved to fear. We are unable, like Moses, to look at so holy a God. Yet, we are able to speak to God, to call God's name in prayer. For God has graciously told us his name.

Because this God reigns in heaven and on earth, God's name is hallowed, holy, since it is to that name that every creature bows—every creature—blue whales, mocking-birds, women and men (Revelation 4–5). Not to know the name of God, not to know how God's name is hallowed, in other words, not to know how to worship, is to live in fundamental conflict with our true selves. We are created for no better purpose than praise. As Saint Augustine said, "because you made us for yourself, our hearts find no peace until they rest in you."

That we do not know how rightly to praise God is obvious. The headlines in this morning's newspaper display our dis-connectedness and disarray. All this killing, stealing, and mayhem, the large evil in which we gleefully engage, as well as the petty nastiness in our relationships with one another are not the sin but rather sin's effects. We are created to praise God, exuberantly to enjoy God. Yet we anxiously attempt to secure our selves by ourselves, frantically seeking to give substance to our lives, failing to acknowledge that a good God has bestowed meaning upon us by God's willingness to be "Our Father." Sin is our singing out of tune.

All creation is meant to hallow the name of God. We must learn the melody of adoration. In learning the Lord's Prayer, we are learning to hallow the name of God, rightly to praise

God. Everything that is exists to praise God's good name. This praise is constitutive of who we are. None of us therefore lives unto ourselves. None of us is, "just a man," or "only one woman," or "merely an accountant." In praying "Our Father," each of us is being commandeered by God, each of us is watching our fate transformed into God's good destiny. We are counting for something in the larger scheme of things, enjoying ourselves being caught up in a larger adventure than the merely private or purely personal, joining our voices with those of all creatures in praising a Holy God who stoops to us, who enjoys our praise, who delights even to hear our songs. The prayer teaches us, in all that we do, to hallow the name of God and, in so doing, we discover our true being.

In praying the Lord's Prayer, we have been commandeered by God, sanctified, set apart, ordained, made holy. We are commissioned to live our lives in such a way as to make visible to all the world that the holy God reigns, that God has a rightful claim to all of his creation, that God has regained some of his rightful territory from the enemy. God's newly won territory is us, those who pray, "Hallowed be thy name."

Thumb through the Psalms and you will note how often the Psalms call Israel and the church to praise. It's as if this were the whole point of the congregation. Praise may not suit our natural inclination. We have to be invited and taught to praise.

> *Praise the LORD!*
> *Praise God in his sanctuary;*
>   *praise him in his mighty firmament!*
> *Praise him for his mighty deeds;*
>   *praise him according to his surpassing greatness!*
>
> *Praise him with trumpet sound;*
>   *praise him with flute and harp!*

Praise him with tambourine and dance;
   praise him with strings and pipe!

Praise him with clanging cymbals;
   praise him with loud clashing cymbals!
Let everything that breathes praise the LORD!
Praise the LORD!

(Psalm 150)

"Holy be your name" is closely related to the following "your kingdom come, your will be done." The fitting response to the holiness of God is our honoring God's name in all that we do and say. Our worship of God, our praise of the holiness of God is linked to ethics, life in the light of the holiness of God.

The Second Vatican Council described Christian worship as "the glorification of God and the sanctification of the faithful." As we glorify God in worship, we are in turn sanctified, made holy in everyday life. Sanctification is a church word that means to be made holy. As we praise God, we become formed in God's image. As Augustine said, "We imitate whom we adore."

In the Sermon on the Mount, Jesus makes the rather astounding claim that we should "be perfect as your father in heaven is perfect" (Matthew 5:48). The word "perfect" here is the Greek word *teleioi*, which we might translate as "the end," in the sense of the goal, the completion, perfection in the sense of ultimate maturation. As we adore the holy God in our worship, we become more holy ourselves. As we pray the Lord's Prayer, we come more closely to resemble the One to whom we pray.

This perfection, moreover, turns out to be about learning to love enemies. *"You have heard that it was said, 'You shall love your neighbor and hate your enemy.' But I say to you, Love your enemies and pray for those who persecute you, so that you may be children of your Father in heaven"* (Matthew 5:43-45).

45

Note Jesus assumes that his disciples will have enemies. Being a Christian involves no presumption that the world is a nice place or that "we can get along by going along." No, being Christian means that you will have enemies you would not have had if you had not been Christian.

Note moreover what makes those enemies is your being part of a community that lives not by violence and enmity but by forgiveness. Christians are first not forgivers, but forgiven. We seek to be reconciled to one another so that our lives make no sense unless they are tied together in one mighty prayer before God. Such reconciliation is possible because we have been forgiven, made righteous, by being given a story for our lives we did not "make up."

Perfection for Christians is the way we talk about our being a people capable of being forgiven without regret. As a people so constituted we can offer our enemies who are real enemies that forgiveness through penance and reconciliation. Yet we are under no illusion that such an offer will make our enemies less our enemies. In fact it may enrage them. Jesus does not say that if we turn our cheek we will not be hit. He just reassures us that if we live as he lived we shall be living the way God rules the world.

Perhaps you thought something like, "Christianity is mostly a matter of trying to do the right thing and to live a good life." But this way of viewing things gets the cart before the horse. Christianity is *not* mainly a matter of what we do and how we live but first a matter of what God in Christ has done. We have no idea of how to live until we first know who God is. So when we say that God's name is holy, that tells us how we ought to live. Knowing the Creator tells us where the creation is meant to move.

Perhaps you are surprised that we did not begin talking about the Christian life by mentioning some ethical dilemma like abortion or drug abuse or capital punishment and then telling you the Christian view on that subject, the correct Christian response to this or that problem.

Note that we began, not with moral problems and ethical dilemmas; we began with prayer. First learn to say these words, learn to pray in this way, learn to have your life bent in this direction. Then you will know how to live. Christians, like Jews, know no strong distinction between our worship and our ethics. We are a people whose moral lives are shaped liturgically. Our ethics is a by-product of our worship. Time and again you can see this dynamic in the Scripture. First Peter sings joyfully, *But you are a chosen race, a royal priesthood, a holy nation, God's own people*. Then, *in order that you may proclaim the mighty acts of him who called you out of darkness into his marvelous light* (1 Peter 2:9).

See the connection? We have been chosen, ordained, adopted as "God's own people" *in order that* we might proclaim God's mighty acts in word and deed.

Again, after telling us that *once you had not received mercy, but now you have received mercy*, 1 Peter immediately demands, *Beloved, I urge you as aliens and exiles to abstain from the desires of the flesh that wage war against the soul. Conduct yourselves honorably* (1 Peter 2:11-12).

You will note the use of strange political designations of Christians as "aliens" and "exiles," even going so far as to call the Christian life "war." The Lord's Prayer is like a bomb ticking in church, waiting to explode and demolish our temples to false gods. It may have slipped past you, but any time you make a statement like "Holy be your name," you have made a revolutionary claim that promises to land you in the middle of conflict, maybe even war.

In the face of this culture's pervasive hedonism, our idolatry of the flag, our worship of ourselves and our assorted deities, give your life to the holy God of Israel whose name is to be hallowed in all that we do and the world will begin calling you "alien" and "exile." Our culture has a way of driving out of the discussion those who do not bow at the culture's altars.

47

When we pray, "Holy be your name," we are both asking God to make his name holy and pledging ourselves not to misuse God's name. This is what the Ten Commandments are getting at when they prohibit our taking God's name "in vain." It is commonplace to hear God's name taken in vain today. Though it may well be blasphemy, saying "God damn" may not be the greatest blasphemy against the name of God. The German soldiers who went into battle in World War II bearing *Gott mit Uns* ("God with Us") on their helmets are a greater blasphemy to the holy name of God. To invoke the name of the free, mighty God as patron of our causes is to take the name of God in vain. Those who are being formed by praying, "Our Father who art in heaven, holy be your name" are not permitted to abuse the holiness of God by attempting to put a leash on God, then dragging God into our crusades and cruelties. The holy God will not be jerked around in this way. So when a president prays a public prayer, calling upon God to bless our troops going into war, that is blasphemy. God's name is not to be used as a rubber stamp for our causes.

It is, after all, a matter of honor. God alone is to be honored. The good news is that the honor we owe God is praise and prayer. Such praise protects us from the false honor—both tempting and destructive—that the world offers us. We so desperately desire status. We so want to be noticed by others without having to notice them in return. Yet in honoring God's name we are giving the only honor worth having. We are thus "saved" from the worldly desire for honor that tempts us to kill in God's name in order to secure honor for ourselves.

One of us knows a college student who is the first person in his family to go to college. When, recently, someone offered this student some illegal drugs saying, "Go ahead, try it. It'll make you feel good," the student replied, "No."

"Don't be so uptight," said the drug dealer. "Nobody is going to know that you tried a little dope, got a little high."

"That's not the point," said the student. "The point is that my mother cleaned houses and washed floors to send me to this college. I am here because of her. I am here for her. I wouldn't do anything that might demean her sacrifice for me."

That comes close to how we are to react to the holy God. Christians don't steal, don't cheat in their marriages, don't bless war, but not in order to get on the good side of God, since, in Christ, we have been made right with God. We are to live in the light of our knowledge of God's name, God's holy name. The conflict we encounter due to our attempts to live faithfully to the gospel doesn't come to us as a surprise. It comes with the territory.

In praying the Lord's Prayer, in naming the holiness of God, we discover not just who God is but also who we are. We are daily reminded that we are not our own. We belong, not to ourselves and our desires, but to God. Thus the Heidelberg Catechism asks the Christian, "What is your only comfort, in life and in death?" The answer? "That I belong—body and soul, in life and in death—not to myself but to my faithful Savior, Jesus Christ." Each of us has been named by the God whom we name in prayer, commandeered, elected, chosen, ordained as priests to the world. We are owned.

We live as we pray.

49

CHAPTER FOUR

"Your kingdom come"

Unexpectedly, quite surprisingly, politics has crept into our Christian praying at this point. Here we were, talking about God, heaven, holiness, and suddenly we find ourselves in the middle of a political argument about a kingdom, transferred to some new place that calls into question the old places in which we have lived. We have not prayed, "Lord, bless our nation" or "Lord protect my family." We pray *your* kingdom come.

Here the Lord's Prayer makes a move toward the specific and the mundane. Be prepared to get even more specific and mundane for we will shortly move, in this prayer, from kingdom, to earth, to bread. In an age in which there is an alleged outburst of enthusiasm for things spiritual, it may come as a shock to admit that Christianity is very materialistic. Our goal is not to fill you with enough spiritual hot air that you float a foot above the earth. Our goal is to teach you to pray in such a way that material matters like politics and bread will be for you spiritual matters. Jesus did not come urging us to think about him, or to feel deeply about him. When he called disciples, he did not come seeking our disembodied individual spirits. Jesus came inviting us to join up with his kingdom. When we see him healing people, casting out demons, we are to know that "the kingdom of God has come upon you."

Now after John was arrested, Jesus came to Galilee, proclaiming the good news of God, and saying " . . . the kingdom of God has come near; repent, and believe in the good news." (Mark 1:14-15)

Seeing the kingdom at hand necessitates a response, a decision. We call this repentance. Will we be part of this kingdom or not? In saying, "Your kingdom come," we are acknowledging that faith in Jesus is not simply an idea or an emotion. It is a concrete reality in which we are to become part or else appear to be out of step with the way things are now that God has come into the world in Jesus. When the kingdom comes, we are "to repent [i.e., change, let go of our citizenship in the old kingdoms] and believe the good news [i.e., join up, become part of the revolution]."

Christianity is forever mixing religion and politics. Jesus is, as the prayer portrays, very "political." To the credit of the rulers of this world, they at least had the good sense to look at Jesus and see that, in him, they were in big trouble. Matthew says that when Jesus was born, the moment King Herod heard about it, he called together his political advisors and *was frightened, and all Jerusalem with him* (Matthew 2:3). Herod had been in office long enough to know a threat to his rule when he saw one. Herod knew that, in this baby at Bethlehem, everything his kingdom was built upon was in mortal peril. So Herod responded in the way rulers usually respond: violence. Herod called out the army and they massacred all the Jewish boy babies (Matthew 2:13-18)—alas, only one of many attempts by governments to rid themselves of Jewish challenges to their power. In praying, "Your kingdom come," we are in a power struggle that can become violent because the kingdoms of the world rarely give up power without a fight.

Early in his earthly ministry, right at the first, even before he preached his first sermon, Jesus was confronted by Satan who offered him complete political control—*all the kingdoms of the world*—if Jesus would only worship him. (Note: Satan is able to offer "all the kingdoms of the world" since they belong to Satan!)

Then the devil led him up and showed him in an instant all the kingdoms of the world. And the devil said to him, "To you I will give their glory and all this authority; for it has been given over to me, and I give it to anyone I please. If you, then, will worship me, it will all be yours." Jesus answered him, "It is written, 'Worship the Lord your God, and serve only him.'" (Luke 4:5-8)

Jesus refused to worship Satan, even if the reward was complete power—as the kingdoms of the world define power. Rather than running the kingdoms of the world, Jesus went about establishing a new kingdom, a kingdom in this world yet not of it—what he called the kingdom of God.

As Luther once said, whatever you would offer your daughter for, that is your god. Most of us would not think of offering up our children to be killed, yet few of us question having our children register for military service. We justify this sacrifice of our children on the basis of our support for American democracy and freedom, but it may be more a matter of worship and prayer.

The story of Jesus' temptation by Satan suggests that kingdom is a question about whom we worship. To be part of this kingdom is to acknowledge who is in charge, whose will ultimately counts in this world. There may be some faiths that detach the individual believer from concern about earthly matters, who strive to rise above outward, visible concerns like swords and shields, wine and bread, politics and power. Christianity is not one of those religions. We want you, body and soul. Indeed, we believe that your body is your soul. So we've got opinions about the way you spend your money, invest your time, cast your ballot.

Kingdoms have boundaries. There are those who are citizens, and there are those who are not. Whereas the prayer addressed to "Our Father," implies a kind of inclusivity, when we pray, "Your kingdom come," we are asserting an exclusivity as well. As Christians, we are not opposed to boundaries. The gap between the world and the kingdom of God ought to be made clear. Those who first met Jesus had the good sense to know that they had encountered one whom they had not met before. Jesus repulsed more people than he attracted.

A certain ruler asked him, "Good Teacher, what must I do to inherit eternal life?" Jesus said to him, "Why do you call me good? No one is good but God alone. You know the commandments: 'You shall not commit adultery; You shall not murder; You shall not steal; You shall not bear false witness; Honor your father and mother.'" He replied, "I have kept all these since my youth." When Jesus heard this, he said to him, "There is still one thing lacking. Sell all that you own and distribute the money to the poor, and you will have treasure in heaven; then come, follow me." But when he heard this, he became sad; for he was very rich. Jesus looked at him and said, "How hard it is for those who have wealth to enter the kingdom of God! Indeed, it is easier for a camel to go through the eye of a needle than for someone who is rich to enter the kingdom of God." (Luke 18:18-25)

What Jesus said and made clear was that he was from somewhere other than our kingdoms. As C. S. Lewis once noted, Jesus spoke and acted in such a way that one either had to follow him or else decide that he was crazy. There was no middle ground in his kingdom. You either had to move toward it, risk letting go and being caught up in his project, or else you had, like the rich ruler, to move on, realizing that

53

you wanted to retain citizenship in the kingdoms of the world.

They were astounded at his teaching, for he taught them as one having authority, and not as the scribes. . . . They were all amazed, and they kept on asking one another, "What is this? A new teaching—with authority! He commands even the unclean spirits, and they obey him." (Mark 1:22, 27)

While we are not opposed to boundaries, God's kingdom enables us to be opposed to the way the world sets up boundaries—on the basis of gender, class, race, economics, or accent. Nothing is more provincial and parochial than the modern nation that sets up national boundaries and then defends them with murderous intensity. God's kingdom's boundaries obliterate all of the world's false means of demarcation between human beings. Here is a kingdom open to all, with no consideration given for the world's boundaries. Our boundary is baptism.

As many of you as were baptized into Christ have clothed yourself with Christ. There is no longer Jew or Greek, there is no longer slave or free, there is no longer male and female; for all of you are one in Christ Jesus. (Galatians 3:27-28)

Baptism is a call to come be citizens of Israel, to become part of God's weird way of saving the world. That weirdness is signified, exemplified, specified in the act of baptism itself. Baptism is Christian initiation.

When you join the Rotary Club, they give you a handshake and a membership card. When you join the church, we throw you into water, bathe you, half drown you, clean you up, and tell you that you have been born again. We thus signify that being a Christian is not natural, not a by-product of being an American. To be Christian is to be adopted by a new nation, the kingdom of God. For the first time in our lives, those old labels and divisions that cause such grief—male/female, slave/free, rich/poor, New Jersey/Texas—are washed away, overcome, not by saying that such divisions don't mean anything, but rather by showing how they have been relativized, subordinated, and washed by our new citizenship. Now, the only division that makes much difference to us is church/world.

To say, "Your kingdom come" is to be willing to become part of the rather weird gathering of strange people, often people whom the world regards as outsiders, who are now on the inside with Jesus. One of the most persistent criticisms of Jesus was the charge that he hung out with disreputable people.

As he sat at dinner in the house, many tax collectors and sinners came and were sitting with him and his disciples. When the Pharisees saw this, they said to his disciples, "Why does your teacher eat with tax collectors and sinners?" But when he heard this, he said, "Those who are well have no need of a physician, but those who are sick." (Matthew 9:10-12)

Every time the church gathers, prays the Lord's Prayer, and eats and drinks the Lord's Supper with Jesus, we show that Jesus continues to be known by the company he keeps at the table. God's kingdom is a bunch of tax collectors, sinners, and sick people eating and drinking with Jesus.

Little about the kingdom of God is self-evident, so don't think that you know all about the kingdom of God just because you are reasonably intelligent. We have people who have been in the church for fifty years who still confess to being shocked by the appearance of God's kingdom when it happens, still get miffed by the people who show up insisting that Jesus has invited them to dinner, are even yet surprised that the light shines in the darkness and the darkness has not overcome it. Perhaps the elusiveness of the kingdom is why most of Jesus' teaching was teaching about the kingdom. Imagine a sermon that begins:

"Blessed are the poor in spirit, for theirs is the kingdom of heaven.
"Blessed are those who mourn, for they will be comforted.
"Blessed are the meek, for they will inherit the earth."
(Matthew 5:3-5)

Blessed are those who are unemployed, blessed are those suffering terminal illness, blessed are those who are going through marital distress.

The congregation does a doubletake. Blessed? Fortunate? Lucky? What kind of world is this? In America, if you are unemployed, people treat you as if you had some sort of disease. They don't want to catch what you have. If your marriage is a failure, you are a failure. That doesn't sound very blessed.

The preacher says, "Wait. I should have been more clear. I wasn't talking about *your* kingdoms, the kingdoms built upon success and achievement and earnest striving. I was talking about the kingdom of God." In this topsy-turvy place, our values are stood on their head. Little in this kingdom comes naturally. It comes because God is in charge and because we are invited to be part of God's rule.

What is that kingdom like? It appears mostly to be known through hints, analogies, parables, and images, rather than by definitions and explanations. In the New Testament, the kingdom is discussed in stories and parables. Jesus said the kingdom is like a little seed that silently grows, eventually yielding great harvest (Mark 4:26-29). The kingdom of God involves a great deal of wasted seed; for many times the seed that is sown fails to take root (Mark 4:1-9). Many times, the kingdom of God appears to the world as something small and insignificant, as small as a mustard seed (Mark 4:30-32), as troublesome a weed as the mustard plant, breaking out all

56

over. The kingdom of God is like a rich man who gave all of his property to his servants and then left town (Mark 13:34-36). In speaking about the kingdom of God mostly in parables, Jesus thereby showed us that the kingdom of God is sometimes difficult for us to see, and tough for him to explain. The kingdom is here, not yet here, surprising, unexpected, threatening, playful, real.

And again he said, "To what should I compare the kingdom of God? It is like yeast that a woman took and mixed in with three measures of flour until all of it was leavened." (Luke 13:20-21)

Note that we pray, "Your kingdom *come*." The kingdom isn't here, not yet in its fullness. God's kingdom is coming. It is here, incipiently, in glimpses, but not in its fullness. This future, now-and-not-yet quality of the Christian faith is known by the word *eschatology* ("talk about last things"). The Christian faith is not satisfied with things as they are, now, today. The Christian faith is not preoccupied with an archaeological exhumation of some distant past by which it attempts to give meaning to an otherwise meaningless present.

The Christian faith is eschatological, always leaning into the future, standing on tiptoes, eager to see what God is bringing to birth among us. We are created for no better purpose than the praise of God. This is our true destiny. Yet any fool can see that the world is not like that, at least not yet. So Christians, in the Lord's Prayer, are busy leaning forward toward that day when all creation shall be fulfilled in one mighty prayer of praise.

Yet we are not merely standing around gazing up into heaven awaiting that future day (Acts 1:11). In praying the Lord's Prayer, we are already participating in that end time. Politics has become prayer. When we pray this prayer, we are thereby signifying our citizenship in this new kingdom offered to all through baptism. We are pledging our allegiance to a new sovereign, relinquishing our allegiance to the

57

kingdoms of this world. As the church gathers to pray this prayer, we are already forming a visible new community, formed on the basis of God's rule rather than on the basis of the way the world holds people together.

This is our end. We use that phrase "the end" in at least two ways. We say "the end" in the sense that this is the end of the line, the last chapter of the story, *finis*. But we also use "the end" in the sense of the purpose of life, that goal toward which we are moving, the end as the point of it all. When we pray the "Lord's Prayer" we are already becoming part of God's promised purpose for the world. We are already, right here and now, being ordered into the hallowing of God's name. We long for the kingdom of God in which God reigns as the one true Lord. We pray that all may recognize God as the one true God. Yet in praying the Lord's Prayer, we are busy becoming as that for which we yearn.

Our talk of an "end"—a goal to which we are moving— ought *not* be understood as a set of ideals we Christians are trying to achieve in the world. Such social activism, which often does much good, can be only another form of atheism, living as if there were no God. Rather what it means to be an eschatological people is to believe that God rules and that we do not have to wait for that rule because God rules in Jesus Christ. Because we have become part of God's rule through our baptism we have been given hope since we can live confident that God's rule is sure, that God's rule is destined to come to all people. To be a people of hope means that we are saved from the world's cynicism. We have been made happy. It means that, in a world as mean and unjust as ours, we Christians can take the time to have a party, a party called worship. It is a great act of faith to be given the grace to let loose and celebrate each Sunday.

"The kingdom of heaven may be compared to a king who gave a wedding banquet for his son. He sent his slaves to call those who had been invited to the wedding banquet, but they would not come.

Again he sent other slaves, saying, 'Tell those who have been invited: Look, I have prepared my dinner, my oxen and my fat calves have been slaughtered, and everything is ready; come to the wedding banquet.' But they made light of it and went away, one to his farm, another to his business, while the rest seized his slaves, mistreated them, and killed them. The king was enraged. He sent his troops, destroyed those murderers, and burned their city. Then he said to his slaves, 'The wedding is ready, but those invited were not worthy. Go therefore into the main streets, and invite everyone you find to the wedding banquet.' Those slaves went out into the streets and gathered all whom they found, both good and bad; so the wedding hall was filled with guests." (Matthew 22:2-10)

The kingdom of God that is coming, here, not here, present, not fully present, is a banquet, a great party thrown for outsiders who, before Jesus, had no place in the promises of God to Israel. By an amazing act of divine generosity, Jesus has made possible a party to which even Gentiles like us have been invited. The kingdom of God is a party to which all of the good people refused the invitation so the host went out and invited all of the bad people. The kingdom of God is a party for a bunch of people with whom we wouldn't be caught dead spending a Saturday night, had we not also been invited.

This is one of the reasons why being in the church can be a real pain, considering the sort of reprobates Jesus has invited to the party, the party that is called kingdom of God.

We are able to live hopefully in a fallen-yet-being-redeemed world because of the One who has taught us to pray "this way." As Christians, to us has been given the grace to know that we live between the times, having seen the fullness of God in Jesus Christ, yet also knowing that all the world is not yet fulfilled as God's world. That tension, stretched as we are between what is ours now in Christ and that which is yet promised, is our role as God's people. We, you and I, are living, breathing evidence that God has not abandoned the world. We are able continually and fervently to pray that God's kingdom come because we know that God's will has been done. We are able to be honest about all the ways in which this world is not the kingdom of God in its fullness and to hope for more because we know that God's will has yet to be done, God's kingdom has yet to come. We are able to live without despair in the world's present situation because, even in us, God has claimed a bit of enemy territory, has wrestled something from the forces of evil and death. That reclaimed, renovated territory is us.

CHAPTER FIVE

"Your will be done, on earth as in heaven"

One of the best stories in the Bible is the story of Joseph and his brothers, told toward the end of Genesis. It is a family story, therefore it is a story about misunderstanding, envy, and violence. Bratty little brother Joseph antagonized his brothers by being Daddy's fair-haired boy. Jacob loved Joseph with unashamed favoritism.

And those dreams! Imagine your kid brother saying, "I had a dream. We were binding sheaves of wheat in the field. And your sheaves all bowed down to my sheaf."

"Really?" said Joseph's brothers.

"Then I dreamed that the sun, the moon, and eleven stars bowed down to me."

"Really?" said the eleven brothers.

"I wonder what Freud would say about my dream?" Joseph asked.

The brothers said to themselves, "We'll give him a dream!" So they plotted against him, attempted to kill him, but eventually settled upon selling little brother Joseph into slavery in Egypt. They bloodied Joseph's coat with sheep's blood, brought the coat to their father saying, "Guess what happened while we were at work today? Something ate little Joseph!"

Through a long series of twists and turns, little brother Joseph, even in his slavery, prospers. His cleverness is recognized by his Egyptian overlords and Pharaoh places Joseph over his holdings. During a great famine, which Joseph predicted through his skill at dream interpretation, Joseph devises and executes a master plan for saving Egypt from hunger.

And who should show up in Egypt looking for food? Joseph's brothers. They do not know that the royal one whom they beg for food is none other than their long forsaken little brother, Joseph. When he finally reveals himself to them, the brothers tremble. They have good reason to be afraid, considering what they tried to do to Joseph. But Joseph says something to his brothers that reassures them and is related to "Your will be done."

Then Joseph said to his brothers, "Come closer to me." And they came closer. He said, "I am your brother, Joseph, whom you sold into Egypt. And now do not be distressed, or angry with yourselves, because you sold me here; for God sent me before you to preserve life. . . . God sent me before you to preserve for you a remnant on earth, and to keep alive for you many survivors. So it was not you who sent me here, but God; he has made me a father to Pharaoh, and lord of all his house and ruler over all the land of Egypt."
(Genesis 45:4-5, 7-8)

Joseph's statement to his brothers is a rather amazing affirmation of the grace and power of God. What seemed like a purely internal family matter, a rather typical story of rivalry and struggle within a troubled family, turns out to be part of a larger story of the realization of God's purposes for the world.

"You meant it for evil—God meant it for good." A story that began with resentment and betrayal turns out to be a story about the preservation of God's people. "You did not send me here," Joseph tells his brothers. They *thought* they were in control as they sold their own brother into slavery. But no, there is something, someone, some deep, loving presence behind the story—some hand greater than the brothers' guilt and evil deeds, some author greater than the actors. The dream lives! The dream of a family through which God will bless the world isn't stumped or thwarted by the brothers.

The bratty little dreamer isn't the hero. The hero of the story, the One who makes it worth retelling is the Author of another plan, a plan hidden but sure. Joseph tells his brothers, "Fear not! What you meant for evil, God meant for good." God's plans will triumph. We're not told *how*. Even the Bible can't do that. We're told that God's plans do triumph.

"God," says Luther, "can shoot with the warped bow and ride the lame horse."

We modern American people are so accustomed to thinking of life as choice or chance. Life is what I do and decide or else life is a roulette wheel of sheer luck. Is that why we often feel so helpless and hopeless? If life is all up to us, then we know enough about ourselves and our brothers and sisters to know we are doomed. A terrible paralysis comes from thinking that it's all up to us. If the fate of the world, the outcome of the future is solely of my doing, or even yours, then—a good freshman course in the history of Western civilization should convince us that we are without hope. No wonder we feel frail and fearful before the bomb, AIDS, the ecological crisis, thinning ozone, or even the department of motor vehicles—it's all choice or chance.

But Joseph, at the end of the story, is able to look back on all the twists and turns of plot and to proclaim, "Fear not! You meant it for evil—God meant it for good." We're not talking about the silly notion that everything that happens, everything you do, occurs because God planned it that way. We're talking about the amazing resilience of God's purposes. God's intent for the world isn't stumped by our plans. God's will *will* be done on earth as it is in heaven.

While not everything that happens in this world happens because God wants it that way—there are still too many murderous brothers and sisters to believe that—sometimes, looking back on your life, the twists and turns, it is amazing how well it all fits, as if there were a hand, an overriding purpose, a divine intent. As God means it to be so.

Saint Augustine said that our lives are like a chicken yard full of random tracks, chicken tracks in the mud, going this way and that in confusion. Seen through the eyes of faith, straining to see the purposes of God, our lives take on pattern, coherence, form; we discover a certain design, a direction as if led by some unseen hand. Then we know with Paul that *all things work together for good for those who love God, who are called according to his purpose* (Romans 8:28). God's will is being done on earth as it is in heaven.

When we pray, "Your will be done on earth as it is in heaven," it may sound at first as if we are urging you to do something—bend your rebellious will to God's will, get busy doing here on earth what God is doing in heaven. While that may be implied—certainly we ought to act in accordance with what is real, and in this prayer, we are saying what is real, namely, the will of a living God—that is not the first thing to be said. "Your will be done, on earth as in heaven" is first a declaration of what God is doing before it implies anything that we ought to do.

In Luther's German translation of the Bible, this phrase is rendered as, *"Dein Wille geschehe, wie im Himmel so auf Erden."* Literally it says, *"Your will appear, as in heaven, so on earth."* This phrase is an earnest longing for God's will to appear in all fullness before us, for God's dealings with the world to appear in convincing clarity and power.

That is one reason why we gather on Sunday and tell stories to one another, stories like the story of Joseph and his brothers. The world is busy telling us stories that say that everything is in our hands, all of it is left up to us. Today we saw an advertisement: "You've got the whole world in your hands—Mastercard." We are the masters of our fate and the captains of our souls. These false stories blind us to the workings of God within the world.

So we gather on a weekly basis and tell stories, pray, and sing, in order that we might better perceive what is really going on in the world, namely, that God is taking our evil and meaning it for good.

When we pray, "Your will be done," we haven't specified a termination date. The world doesn't have to come out right for us tomorrow. One of the problems we have with waiting for the will of God to be fulfilled is waiting. We want what we want and we want it now. Yet, as 2 Peter says, *with the Lord one day is as a thousand years, and a thousand years are as one day* (2 Peter 3:8). Sometimes, one of the main functions of our prayer is to give us something useful to do in the meantime. While we are waiting for God's will to appear, we pray. When it comes to the will of God, sometimes the most important thing to pray for is patience.

We have just prayed, "your kingdom come," a petition full of *hope*. Now we are taught to say, "your will be done," a petition for *patience*. That the virtues of hope and patience should be so joined is not surprising for a people on a journey called kingdom. Indeed our hopes as Christians can make us dangerous if they are not schooled by patience. Without patience we are tempted to storm the walls of injustice, destroying our enemy and thus betraying God's way of forgiveness. Instead we are called to be a patient people schooled as we are by the patience of our crucified God so that the world may know that love, not violence, rules this world. God's way of dealing with us and our evil is called the cross, the unlimited, suffering patience of God. We are called to take up our cross and follow God's patience.

Accordingly, when we pray, "Your will be done," we are not asking that things come out right as we want things to

65

come out, but rather we are asking that God's will be done. Too often, we are conditioned to think of prayer as asking God for what we want—dear God, give me this, give me that. But now, in praying that God's will be done on earth as it is in heaven, we are attempting to school ourselves to want what God wants. We receive, not what our hearts desire, but rather we become so enthralled with a vision of what God is doing on earth and in heaven, that we forget the story that the world has told us—that we have nothing better to do than to satisfy our desires.

We live in a society of omnivorous desire. Prayer can be risky in such an environment. In our culture, everything—all philosophies, psychologies, all people and things—are reduced to techniques, methods of getting what our hearts desire. Our culture is a vast supermarket of desire in which we are encouraged constantly to consume.

Many of us learn, in such a culture, that getting "what I want" is not simply a matter of not having enough money to fulfill all my desires. "What I want" becomes unattainable—there is an ever-rising threshold of expectation in which, the more we get, the more we want, so we are never satisfied. Getting "what I want" is also a matter of not having the resources to know for sure what it is I want.

So we lurch from this experience to that, try on this mask or that one, switch friends, grope for new thrills, buy this, drink that, all in a frantic, never-ending attempt to "Get what I want," fearful that we might miss the one experience that would really make our lives worth living.

"Getting what I want" is related to my knowledge of my real self, my imagination or lack of it, the range of my experience and wisdom. Therefore it is absolutely essential, as the Lord's Prayer moves toward asking God for things, that we begin by asking God that God's will might appear to us, might be made manifest to our eyes in all of its terrible and wonderful distance from what we want.

66

To pray, "Your will be done," is to beg, not for what we want, but rather to beg to have our lives caught up in some project greater than our lives. Here, in our prayer, we, like Joseph and his brothers, have our lives caught up in something bigger and better than our lives, namely, the adventure of what God is doing in the world.

Standing on a battleship in 1945, President Truman was handed a note telling him that the atomic bomb had been dropped on Hiroshima. "This is the greatest thing in the history of the world," Truman told the sailors standing near him.

Truman was wrong. The bomb was only one more chapter in the old, depressingly same story of inhumanity and godlessness. The greatest thing that happened in the history of the world took place a long time before the bomb at a place called Calvary. The greatest thing in the history of the world is when God's will is done.

We pray in the conviction that God's will *has* been done "on earth as in heaven." Our wills and our relentless, murderous execution of them nailed Jesus to the cross. God's will, and God's determination to have his will done on earth as in heaven, appeared on the cross. The cross was the ultimate, determinative clash between our wills and God's will. In the cross of Christ, God met the principalities and powers and exposed and then disarmed them. Even though the war between God and the forces of evil continues—in cancer wards, in Bosnia and Serbia, in famine, at the Pentagon, in our words and actions every day—the decisive battle has been fought and won. God's will has been done, though the consequences of that decisive act continue to be played out among us.

Let us say again that heaven is not some place "up there." Heaven is that place where God is and where we are totally with God, wherever God's "communion of saints" takes place, wherever God's will appears in explicit fullness and undeniable power. On Sunday, in the Eucharist, the Lord's

Supper, it is like a window to heaven where we catch at least a glimpse of what it is like to feast eternally with God. This God invites us to the Lord's Table on Sunday so that we might begin to learn the moves required to feast at God's table forever. Our communion now, here is a witness to the world to God's intention that his will be done everywhere "on earth." No corner of creation has been abandoned by God to sin and the devil. We pray, praise, and eat together in order to show to the world that there is no corner of creation (even here!) where God's will is not being done, even in those areas where God is not acknowledged as God. The world, sinful as it often is, is still *God's* world where God's will is being done.

As the police moved in to break up a demonstration, someone among the demonstrators shouted, "Quick, everyone to your knees, let's pray!"

Someone began to shout above the confusion, "Our Father, who art in heaven, hallowed be thy name. Thy kingdom come, thy will be done, on earth as it is in heaven. . . . "

The charging police faltered. Some of the police instinctively joined in the prayer. Suddenly, the peace demonstration had taken on new meaning. An angry confrontation between a group of dissidents and the police was being opened up into something of wider significance. The will of God was appearing; the principalities and powers were being exposed. Religion was becoming explicitly political; politics was getting mixed up with prayer.

There can never be any question of whether or not Christians ought to withdraw from the world. Here, in praying, "Your will be done on earth . . ." we are being thrust into the world, for there is nowhere else that we will be able to see God's will appearing other than in the world. If someone has come to prayer, hoping to find some sort of escape hatch from the struggles of the world, here the prayer thrusts us back into the heart of the fray.

It is all very public. Note that the Lord's Prayer is meant to be prayed aloud, as a public gesture. Rarely do we mumble this prayer quietly. It is meant to be a very audible, very public event. As we have said, this is one of the most defiant, politically charged, public things we Christians can do—pray the Lord's Prayer.

Yet in praying the Lord's Prayer, and in living this prayer, we Christians may seem strange and foreign to the world. Sometimes the world, upon hearing the Lord's Prayer prayed, in front of Caesar's images, on the steps of the court house, before a high school graduation, even in church on a Sunday, has sought to drive Christians out of the world, but that is the world's doing, an attempt to exclude us arising out of the world's own insecurity. We have nowhere else to pray this prayer than in the world.

Again, to pray *"Your* will be done" is to recognize that prayer is about achieving God's will, not our will. Jesus fervently prayed to be delivered from arrest and death in the Garden of Gethsemane (Matthew 26:39). Jesus got "no" for an answer to his prayer. Paul prayed to be delivered out of his "thorn in the flesh," some sort of physical disability, many times (2 Corinthians 12:7). Paul was delivered only in death.

The ending of all truly Christian prayer is the same that Jesus prayed in Gethsemane: *Not my will but yours be done.*

Prayer in Jesus' name is lifelong training in taking God's will a little more seriously and our own will a little less so.

CHAPTER SIX

"Give us today our daily bread"

Any notion that Christianity is some sort of otherworldly trip into never-never land is dispelled by the time the Lord's Prayer gets down to the nitty-gritty and boldly asks for bread. The act of asking for bread is for us a daily reminder that our lives, like our bread, are gifts from God. Daily we are dependent upon God. Just like the Hebrews in the wilderness who would have starved had not God sent the gift of manna (Exodus 16:1-36), so we would perish were it not for the daily, mundane, essential gifts of God. We therefore are bold to ask God for daily bread.

Furthermore, amid all the talk about heaven and God, the prayer now reminds us that we are fleshly people who live by bread. Salvation is the realization not only that our lives are gifts but that our lives are daily dependent upon and constituted by bread, which this prayer has taught us to regard as a gift. Our God loves to feed us.

As he went ashore, he saw a great crowd; and he had compassion for them, because they were like sheep without a shepherd; and he began to teach them many things. When it grew late, his disciples came to him and said, "This is a deserted place, and the hour is now very late; send them away so that they may go into the surrounding country and villages and buy something for themselves to eat." But he answered them, "You give them something to eat." They said to him, "Are we to go and buy two hundred denarii worth of bread, and give it to them to eat?" And he said to them, "How many loaves have you? Go and see." When they had found out, they said, "Five, and two fish." Then he ordered them to get all the people to sit down in groups on the green grass. So they sat down in groups of hundreds and of fifties. Taking the five loaves and the two fish, he looked up to heaven, and blessed and broke the loaves, and gave them to his disciples to set before the people; and he divided the two fish among them all. And all ate and were filled. (Mark 6:34-42)

Jesus is the one who has compassion on hungry people, the Savior for whom hunger is an affront to the inbreaking kingdom of God, the host who feeds us, and the teacher who commands us, "You give them something to eat."

Israel would know its Messiah, said Isaiah, at the table. When Messiah comes, those who are hungry will be fed. The expected kingdom of God is a meal for the hungry and the forgotten. On that day, says the prophet, there will come forth in all the earth the great shout:

> *Ho, everyone who thirsts,*
> *come to the waters;*
> *and you that have no money,*
> *come, buy and eat!*
> *Come, buy wine and milk*
> *without money and without price.*
> (Isaiah 55:1)

In one of his sermons, Augustine says something to the effect that, when the priest prays before the bread on the altar on Sunday, it is not that the priest is saying that, by virtue of this prayer, this ordinary bread is now transformed into a sacrament strange and extraordinary. It is rather that, in praying the Prayer of Thanksgiving at the altar, the priest

71

acknowledges bread as a gift of a loving God and therefore that it is holy, a sacrament.

A person participating in that prayer might say, "That bread upon the altar looks suspiciously like the bread that I had for breakfast this morning. At breakfast, I did not think of that bread as holy."

"Right," says the church. "That's the point. Now, after praying this prayer over bread at church on Sunday, perhaps you will eat your bread differently on Monday."

The church is always teaching us, through this prayer, that our lives are fragile, dependent creations and that God cares about all of that. God gives us what we need, even something so mundane, but utterly essential, as bread.

Yet the bread of breakfast is different from the bread that is the body of our Lord in the Eucharist. At the Lord's Supper by faith we are made participants in God's body so that the world may know that the world is storied through God's presence. We are subsumed into the adventure of God's salvation of the world. Through this meal God unites us with one another in a mystical bond. We call this a mystery not because by this meal our intelligence is confounded, but because the more we understand God's unrelenting love, the love embodied and made manifest in this meal, the deeper the mystery such love evokes.

In the Eucharist we are faced with reality that confounds our speech. It is a reality too true to be a mere matter of noble ideas and religious inclinations. This faith does its business in bread and wine. This God transforms all of our lives, even the most earthy and ordinary of our lives, into signs of divine presence. So when asked what we believe about God, we Christians tend to point to a group of former strangers eating together around a table as family called Eucharist. Or we take you to a dark river where folk are descending into the waters, dying to their old selves, rising as new creations, called baptism. The table, a loaf of bread, the bath, all become expressions of the way our Lord has intruded upon the world, claiming it as his own.

On Easter, two despondent disciples walked together toward the little village of Emmaus. A stranger joins them on the road, asking them why they look so depressed.

"Are you the only person in Jerusalem who hasn't heard the things that have taken place this weekend?" Then they told him about the death of Jesus that had occurred three days before.

Then,

As they came near the village to which they were going, he walked ahead as if he were going on. But they urged him strongly, saying, "Stay with us, because it is almost evening and the day is now nearly over." So he went in to stay with them. When he was at table with them, he took bread, blessed and broke it, and gave it to them. Then their eyes were opened, and they recognized him.
(Luke 24:28-31a)

When we want to meet God, we Christians do not go up some high mountain, do not rummage around in our psyches, do not hold hands, close our eyes, and sing "Kum Ba Yah" in the hope of revelation. We gather and break bread in Jesus' name. That's where he has chosen to meet us, that's where our eyes are opened and we recognize him. We pray "Give us this day our daily bread," not just as a survival strategy; no matter how much bread we get, we shall not survive. In praying for daily bread we are praying for daily presence of God among us.

Note that we pray only for *daily* bread. A more accurate translation of this word "daily" might be *sufficient* or *enough*. To pray for more would tempt us to try to live as if we were other than those who live only by the will and working of a gracious God. When manna was given in the wilderness, the Hebrews were permitted to gather only as much as they needed for each day (Exodus 16:16). Daily we must reach out

73

to God who daily reaches out to us. Daily we wake up to the realization that, if we are here, if our lives have significance and substance, it is only because of the daily gifts of God.

A group of students were spending a week at a Trappist monastery. At the evening meal, enjoying in silence the wonderful, delicious bread, one of the students blurted out, "Hey, did we make this bread or did somebody give it to us?"

One of the monks answered, "Yes."

We live in a society that abhors dependence upon God or anyone else. Yet every time we ask God for bread, we are acknowledging not only our dependence upon a beneficent God but also our dependence on other people. No bread comes to our table without the work, the sacrifice, and the gifts of strangers whom we do not know, and cannot thank.

Our society teaches us to attempt to be self-sufficient, autonomous, freestanding, on our own. Thus the Lord's Prayer, being so clearly against our natural inclinations, must be prayed daily, even as we need food daily. Sometimes we think those who are actually hungry, those who are really poor, may be ahead of us in this realization. Those who have so little are better able to see our utter dependence, the necessity of our having to pray "give us this day." They have learned to pray with others, for the gifts that can only come from others, because their poverty has taught them that our lives are lived as gifts. Perhaps that is why Jesus proclaimed the poor and the hungry to be at the very center of his kingdom.

> *Then he looked up at his disciples and said:*
> *"Blessed are you who are poor,*
> *for yours is the kingdom of God.*
> *"Blessed are you who are hungry now,*
> *for you will be filled."*
> (Luke 6:20-21*a*)

At this point the prayer ought to move us toward honest confession. Let's face it. Most of us don't think much about daily bread because, for most of us, at least the people who will read this book, bread is not a problem. Most of us perish from too much bread rather than too little, filling the gnawing emptiness within through ceaseless consumption. We are rich and, as we have noted, in the Scripture, rich people are in big trouble.

A woman in a little village in Honduras trudges up the mountain each day to gather and then carry down the mountain the sticks for her cooking fire. She then goes back up the mountain to fetch water for cooking the food. Then she grinds the corn her husband has raised, cherishing every kernel, hoping that this season's corn will last through the winter. The tortillas are made in the palm of her hand. She drops them in the pan, cooks them and feeds them one-by-one to her children, the only food they will have that day to fill their aching stomachs. That woman undoubtedly prays, "Give us this day our daily bread" differently from the way we pray that petition.

For us, we ought to pray for the grace to be able to say, in a culture of overconsumption, "Give us the grace to know when enough is enough" or "Help us to say, 'No' when the world entices us with so much." In praying this prayer, perhaps we will learn to "get back to basics," perhaps we will become schooled in desiring what we really need rather than that which we desire. Perhaps we will one day be able to say with Paul:

I have learned to be content with whatever I have. I know what it is to have little, and I know what it is to have plenty. In any and all circumstances I have learned the secret of being well-fed and of going hungry, of having plenty and of being in need. I can do all things through him who strengthens me. (Philippians 4:11b-13)

Centuries ago, Gregory of Nyssa noted the wonder that, in the Lord's Prayer, when one considers all that we need, the only thing we are permitted to ask for is something so basic as bread. Not herds or silken robes, not a prominent position, monuments or statues. Only bread.

At the beginning of this book, we noted the significance of praying "Our Father." Note here that we pray, "Give us our bread." We are not praying for my bread; it's our bread. Bread is a communal product. No bread is eaten alone. The farmers in Iowa, the bakers in New York, the delivery truck drivers in your hometown all make bread a corporate endeavor. None of us eats or lives alone.

That implies that bread is not only a communal product but it is also a corporate responsibility. St. Basil the Great made explicit in a sermon that nothing that belongs to us is ours alone, particularly that which we have in excess of "our daily bread":

> The bread that is spoiling in your house belongs to the hungry. The shoes that are mildewing under your bed belong to those who have none. The clothes stored away in your trunk belong to those who are naked. The money that depreciates in your treasury belongs to the poor!

Our bread is not ours to hoard. Our bread belongs to our sisters and brothers. Bread is God's gift which, like so many other good gifts of God, we pervert by our selfishness. To pray, "Give us today our daily bread," is to radically reexamine ourselves, to acknowledge the claim that God has placed upon us through the gift of bread, to admit the responsibility we have for our neighbor's need.

So as you learn to pray this prayer, note that you necessarily offer your life to others. Put as offensively as we know how, Christianity is about your money, about economics. Salvation is material. Certainly, spirituality is about material things, but we believe nothing is more "spiritual" than money. Through learning to pray this prayer we are taught that our money is not "ours." Thus we can be asked to share because what we have is shared.

For example, the church may well ask us to tell one another how much we make a year. If the church were to ask us this, we would respond, "But that is private!" Unfortunately, privacy is not a Christian category. We are saved from our privacy by being made part of people who can tell us what we should do with our money, with our genitals, with our lives. This is the "good news," which is gospel—that we no longer have to fear one another or ourselves. We have been made part of a good company, a wonderful adventure, so that we no longer need "mine." You may well think at this point the prayer is hitting too close to home. Things are getting serious. But we did not warn you that it was dangerous to pray this prayer?

CHAPTER SEVEN

"Forgive us our sins as we forgive those who sin against us"

In the riots following the first Rodney King verdict, Reginald Denny was dragged from his truck and viciously beaten by a raging gang. After his painful recovery, he met face to face with his attackers, shook hands with them, and forgave them. A reporter, commenting on the scene, wrote, "It is said that Mr. Denny is suffering from brain damage."

Can we agree that forgiveness is an outrageous human act? In our society where might makes right, a society of a myriad of victims, each licking his or her cherished wounds, forgiveness seems crazy. Furthermore, there are many misunderstandings of what Christians mean when we speak of forgiveness. So right here is where the Lord's Prayer is most difficult to pray. Perhaps that is why this is the longest and the most involved petition in the Lord's Prayer. As usual, it first asks God to do something for us. Then it promises that we will do something for others. Before there is any talk in the prayer about our forgiving anyone else, we are made to ask for forgiveness ourselves. Before there is any consideration of the wrongs that we have suffered, we are made to ponder the great wrong God has suffered through us.

In the prayer, we begin by asking for bread and so quickly move to the outrageous petition to be forgiven for our debts. When Luke records this prayer, Luke says:

And forgive us our sins,
for we ourselves forgive
everyone indebted to us.
             (Luke 11:4*a*)

Matthew says: *And forgive us our debts,* as we also have forgiven our debtors (Matthew 6:12). There are reasons for thinking that Matthew's "debts" is closer to Jesus' Aramaic words. Though there is a long historical tradition of saying "trespasses" here, that is not found in the New Testament. The first meaning of "debts" is the plain economic sense that there are those who owe us money. Before we get metaphorical with this word "debts," we ought to try out its literal economic meaning. What would it take for us to be the sort of people who were free enough to forgive the debts that we are owed? Have you ever forgiven a debt that someone owed you?

Saying "debts" gives a nice specificity to our petition. Note that the prayer realistically assumes that we do have debts. Our books are in the red, as far as our relationship to God is concerned. We have run up a debt with God so large that all we can do is ask for forgiveness. We can never hope to pay it back. Once we begin boldly asking God for things, we don't hold back. Having acknowledged our utter dependence upon God for daily necessities like bread, now we acknowledge our utter dependence upon God to forgive us the debt we cannot repay.

A friend of ours, whose wife is an attorney, once visited his wife at work in a bankruptcy court. As the court begins, before the particular case is to be heard, the bailiff cries out, "All debtors rise."

That's us.

If we say that we have no sin, we deceive ourselves, and the truth is not in us (1 John 1:8).

We wish that the prayer said something to God like, "Teach us to forgive others, so that we might also be forgiven." But it doesn't. The prayer knows that we would love to conceive of ourselves first as forgivers. This would leave us in control. From our great store of righteousness, we could reach out in love to those who had injured and wronged us. No, first the prayer asks us to ask to be forgiven. That takes us out of control. It means that we are suddenly at the mercy of someone else's account of our lives rather than our own.

To be out of control can mean many things, but for Christians it means we must recognize our status as creatures. We don't create our lives; we are not the sole authors of the stories that constitute our lives. Rather to be out of control means we must recognize that we are characters in God's story. Moreover when we deny our storied character we live in fundamental contradiction to who we were created to be. That condition is what we must learn to call sin.

Prayer is the essential practice, the gift that God has given us to help us rediscover the joy of being a creature, of being out of control. That is what is meant by being graced—even in our sin, God refuses to abandon us. So we discover our true nature by learning to accept God's good gift without regret. This may sound too easy, but it is anything but that.

For example, if an acquaintance gives you a gift you had not expected, you find you are in an awkward situation. If it is a gift which, in receiving, you realize that you really want, that you do not wish to refuse, you feel at a disadvantage. This, after all, is an acquaintance, not a close friend, and this person has given you a gift that you did not know you wanted but which you now "need." Many of us immediately seek to give something in return because we know gift giving and receiving is a game of power and we fear "owing" the gift giver. Is it any wonder we hate God since we fear One who gives and for whom there is nothing we can give in return? All God asks in return is that we enjoy our worship of our true Lord.

The Gospels are the story of Jesus as God's gift of forgiveness. Notice, for example, how often Jesus forgives people, particularly in the Gospel of John. They ask to be healed, he forgives them. They ask for an explanation of his teaching, he forgives them. "Who is this who forgives sins?" his critics asked. In forgiving, he not only demonstrated his divinity, but also forced us to acknowledge our dependency.

It is the nature of this God to forgive, not because our God is soft on sin, but because our God is determined to have a family, is committed to have us.

The LORD is merciful and gracious,
slow to anger and abounding in steadfast love.
He will not always accuse,
nor will he keep his anger forever.
He does not deal with us according to our sins,
nor repay us according to our iniquities.
For as the heavens are high above the earth,
so great is his steadfast love toward those who fear him;
as far as the east is from the west,
so far he removes our transgressions from us.
As a father has compassion for his children,
so the LORD has compassion for those who fear him.
(Psalm 103:8-13)

To reach out for forgiveness means that I am not the sole author of my life story. Nothing assaults the contemporary understanding of our lives more than to ask for forgiveness. Indeed, in putting forgiveness on the table for consideration, I have now learned that it is precisely my sinful desire to be the sole author of my life that creates my debts. So we are asked in this petition to come out from behind our facade, to become exposed, vulnerable, empty-handed, to risk reconciliation to the one who has the power to forgive us.

To do so is to learn the painful but liberating truth that our lives are not our own.

Furthermore, we say "Forgive us our sins as we forgive those who sin against us." The plural is significant. We are conditioned to think of sin as a personal problem, a private slipup. Yet the most interesting sins we commit are utterly corporate and communal.

Forgiveness may be the most political act Christians possess. We inherit practices from the past based upon terrible injustices and evil. For instance, America is a country whose history is forever marred by slavery. Race remains an insoluble problem because those who are White, cannot do anything about the past other than to forget it. What do you do about actions that are so wrong that nothing can be done to make them right? As a result, African Americans and Whites seem to be caught in an unending game of exaggerated guilt and self-righteousness.

We believe that one of the most extraordinary signs of God's grace is the willingness of African American Christians to seek reconciliation with White Christians. That African Americans remain Christian at all is a miracle since they were told that Christianity justified slavery. What could be more powerful than for White Christians to accept the forgiveness offered by realizing that we need not deny the sins of the past? Rather, now our memories can be redeemed through the confession of sin so that our stories, as Whites and as Blacks can be transformed into the common story of being Christian.

All have sinned and fall short of the glory of God (Romans 3:23).

We are also taught to pray that if we are to be forgiven for our debts, then we can truly be forgivers. The one who has experienced forgiveness is the one best able to forgive. Sometimes the church presents the gospel as if Christians are people who are eager to forgive, just dying to do good. Yet here we see that Christians are not tingling masses of availability ready to do a good deed or to forgive their enemies. Jesus told some great stories about this.

Then Peter came and said to him, "Lord, if another member of the church sins against me, how often should I forgive? As many as seven times?" Jesus said to him, "Not seven times, but, I tell you, seventy-seven times.

"For this reason the kingdom of heaven may be compared to a king who wished to settle accounts with his slaves. When he began the reckoning, one who owed him ten thousand talents was brought to him; and, as he could not pay, his lord ordered him to be sold, together with his wife and children and all his possessions, and payment to be made. So the slave fell on his knees before him, saying, 'Have patience with me, and I will pay you everything.' And out of pity for him, the lord of that slave released him and forgave him the debt. But that same slave, as he went out, came upon one of his fellow slaves who owed him a hundred denarii; and seizing him by the throat, he said, 'Pay what you owe.' Then his fellow slave fell down and pleaded with him, 'Have patience with me, and I will pay you.' But he refused; then he went and threw him into prison until he would pay the debt. When his fellow slaves saw what had happened, they were greatly distressed, and they went and reported to their lord all that had taken place. Then his lord summoned him and said to him, 'You wicked slave! I forgave you all that debt because you pleaded with me. Should you not have had mercy on your fellow slave, as I had mercy on you?'" (Matthew 18:21-33)

The great Christian writer George Herbert said, "He that cannot forgive others, breaks the bridge over which he himself must pass if he would ever reach heaven; for every one has need to be forgiven." Our forgiveness begins as a response to our being forgiven. It is not so much an act of generosity toward our fellow offending human beings as an act of gratitude toward our forgiving God.

This is nothing like the superficial "I'm OK, you're OK." In forgiving us and asking us to forgive others, God is not saying, "There, there, your sin is really not such a big deal after all." So many of our human gatherings are superficial because we lack the means to forgive one another when genuine wrong is done. Lacking a means of forgiveness, all we can do is to say, in effect, "I will promise to stay out of your life and affirm what you do if you promise to stay out of my life and affirm me." Christian forgiveness is not cheap. Our sin is consequential. Rather, in forgiving us, God is refusing to hold our sin against us, God is refusing to let our sin have the last word in the way the world is moving.

In commanding us to forgive others, Jesus is not saying that the injustice we have suffered is inconsequential. The sin we commit causes pain. The sins committed against us cause pain. Rather, Jesus is refusing to let sin have the last word in our story. In commanding us to forgive, Jesus is not producing a race of doormats, a new set of victims who, having been slapped on the right cheek, offer the left as well so that they may be twice victimized. Jesus has no interest in producing victims; the world produces enough.

Rather, in commanding us to forgive, Jesus is inviting us to take charge, to turn the world around, to throw a monkey wrench in the eternal wheel of retribution and vengeance. We don't have silently to suffer the hurt, to lick our wounds, lying in wait for the day when we shall at last be able to return the blow that was dealt to us. We can take charge, turn things around, be victors rather than victims. We can forgive.

The courage to forgive one another begins in the humility engendered by the realization that we have been forgiven. Forgiveness is a gift, a gift that is first offered to us, before we can offer it to others. So every Sunday the church reminds us that we gather as those who have been forgiven, for that is the way we plan to produce heroic souls who are able to forgive.

A pastor told us of a man who had been on the outs with the church since his adolescence. Finally, after his family had pleaded with him to try church again, he gets up the nerve to go to church. He wanders into an Episcopal church during the middle of the service when the congregation is on its knees praying the Prayer of Confession, "We have done those things which we ought not to have done and we have left undone those things which we ought to have done . . . ."

and he smiles and says, "Good! Sounds just like my kind of crowd."

We pray as the forgiven and the unforgiving, as those who have been spectacularly forgiven and loved by Christ on the cross yet who are ridiculously unforgiving and unloving when it comes to the wrongs we suffer from others. He alone can command us, as he commanded Peter, to forgive seventy-times-seven times because, at last count, he has forgiven us about seventy-times-seven trillion times.

In our forgiving and being forgiven, we are made part of God's new age through which we learn the purpose of our creation. We are swept up into God's adventure called the kingdom, we become part of God's defeat of the powers that would otherwise dominate our lives. If you have ever been forgiven by someone, you know the way in which that forgiveness frees you, releases you in a way that is close to divine. If you have ever forgiven someone who wronged you greatly you know how such forgiveness is not cheap and how forgiving someone who has wronged you is a way of breaking the hold of that wrong upon your life. You can breathe. Even more than this freedom and grace that comes from forgiveness is the realization that, in our forgiveness of those "who have trespassed against us," we are enabled to participate in some of the divine energy that was released in the world when God in Christ forgave us for what we did to God's Son.

Forgiveness is not natural. That's why we have to pray, "Forgive us our sins as we forgive those who sin against us" every day. After the bombing in Oklahoma City, there was a city-wide memorial service. Billy Graham spoke at the service. He began by saying, "We are here with you to let the healing begin. We are here to show you that a nation stands beside you in your grief. We are here to forgive."

We daresay that few present that day were there to forgive. The attorney general was talking retribution; the president was promising the death penalty. Dr. Graham was speaking out of the peculiarity, the specificity of the Christian faith, which teaches us, on a regular basis, to pray, "Forgive us our sins as we forgive those who sin against us" until we are able to pray these words by heart.

We do not have to be great fans of Dr. Graham to see his willingness to call for forgiveness even amid the horror of Oklahoma City as strong testimony to the power of the cross. We can offer forgiveness because we must be forgiven. After all, the terror that we perpetrated there began in our society's easy acceptance of the violence that we call "war" or "national defense." The people accused of perpetrating the bombing in Oklahoma City had been members of the United States military. There they learned the assumption that violence in a good cause is legitimate.

The powers that continue to misshape lives through violence were decisively unmasked and defeated in the cross of Christ. There their weakness was forever exposed as they were brought to heel through Christ's submission to their power. Yet he triumphed through God's resurrecting him from the dead. Without that resurrection the forgiveness offered by Dr. Graham is a lie. But we know, as Dr. Graham knows, that Christ sits at the right hand of the Father, making possible for us to pray through the Spirit, "Forgive us our sins as we forgive those who sin against us."

And when you were dead in trespasses . . . God made you alive together with him, when he forgave us all our trespasses, erasing the record that stood against us with its legal demands. He set this aside, nailing it to the cross. He disarmed the rulers and authorities and made a public example of them, triumphing over them in it.
(Colossians 2:13-15)

CHAPTER EIGHT

"Save us from the time of trial and deliver us from evil"

The Christian life is no safe harbor, secure from storms and struggle. Those who are members of this promised kingdom are, with Christ, at war with the powerful. We are thus those who pray to be saved.

And when he got into the boat, his disciples followed him. A windstorm arose on the sea, so great that the boat was being swamped by the waves; but he was asleep. And they went and woke him up, saying, "Lord, save us! We are perishing!"
(Matthew 8:23-25)

Christians are those who ask to be saved. When we pray to God to save us, we are not asking for some changed self-understanding, some new way of feeling about ourselves, something to put zest in our lives. Salvation in Christ is being adopted (baptism), made members of a people, Israel, and the church. We really believe that if we were not part of this people we could not be saved.

So when the church has opinions about how you spend your money, how you have sex, how you vote, this is salvation. You are not simply being saved from personal greed or licentiousness, you are thereby being made a member of God's people.

Note that we don't pray, "Save *me.*" It's, "Save *us.*" Certainly, the "me" is included in the "us." Just as we began by praying, "Our Father," so here we find again that we are being included in a larger drama (salvation) that is more determinative of who you are than any available "me." You join all those saints through the ages who have had their lives transformed, commandeered, turned over, and detoxified by the love of God in Christ. Like the disciples in Matthew 8, we are all in the same boat, tossed by a storm not of our creation, praying, "Lord, save us!"

Pray in the Spirit at all times in every prayer and supplication. To that end keep alert and always persevere in supplication for all the saints. Pray also for me, so that when I speak, a message may be given to me to make known with boldness the mystery of the gospel, for which I am an ambassador in chains. Pray that I may declare it boldly, as I must speak. (Ephesians 6:18-20)

Words like "save" and "trial" and "deliver" are words of crisis. They remind us that to pray this prayer means to be thrust into the middle of a cosmic struggle. At this point the temperature rises within the Lord's Prayer. Things are not right in the world. It is as if something, someone has organized things against God. You pray this prayer faithfully, attempting to align your life to it and the next thing you know, it's like you are under assault.

How often is salvation presented as some sort of helpful solution to everything that ails us. "Lonely? Come to Jesus and get that fixed." "Alcoholic? Come to Jesus and be delivered of your addiction." "Confused? Join the church and find all the answers." In such a presentation of the gospel, salvation is the resolution of all your problems, the way to fix whatever ails you.

But this petition, in which we ask for salvation, deliverance, and help in time of trial reminds us that salvation in Christ is an adventure, a journey, a larger drama. Praying this prayer is the beginning of problems we would never have had had we not met Christ and enlisted with Christ's people. The forces of evil do not relinquish their territory without a fight and, in being saved, God's newly won territory is you.

You become a virtual battleground where the living God fights the powers. So praying this prayer is a bit like war:

Finally, be strong in the Lord and in the strength of his power. Put on the whole armor of God, so that you may be able to stand against the wiles of the devil. For our struggle is not against enemies of blood and flesh, but against the rulers, against the authorities, against the cosmic powers of this present darkness, against the spiritual forces of evil in the heavenly places. Therefore take up the whole armor of God, so that you may be able to withstand on that evil day, and having done everything, to stand firm.
(Ephesians 6:10-13)

In praying that God will not "put us to the test," we pray that God will not make us vulnerable to those powers that rage against God's kingdom. What you are up against, in being saved, is not simply your personal faults and foibles, your petty temptations and peccadilloes. You are up against what we call "the principalities and powers." Evil is large, cosmic, organized, subtle, pervasive, and real. The powers never appear as evil or coercive. The powers always masquerade as freedoms that we have been graciously given or as necessities that we cannot live without.

For example, "the economy" is a power. We have been taught to believe that there is some autonomous, freestanding reality that is called "the economy," which is determinative of our lives, which can make us glad or sad, and which is worth our most frantic efforts and deepest dedication. "Wall Street has decided" we sometimes hear and say.

Another power is "race," which we describe as a reality that determines a person's fate, the person's outlook on life, and is the source of all meaning and value. "Gender" is another power. The world tells us, when face-to-face with the powers, our main job is to adapt and to adjust. After a bombing raid in the war with Iraq, a general was asked why so many people were killed. The reply, "National defense required it." End of discussion. Those are powers.

"The media" are a power. It appears to be good—we need information, don't we? From morning until night, "the media" feed us images, facts, names, sights and sounds that determine our angle of vision. "The media" offer to tell us what is going on in the world, what is and what is not. We call it "news."

Yet in praying this prayer, you have joined in a battle over what is. What is "news"? Who defines "reality"? Through what metaphors and images will we describe the world? In any given week, something like fifty million Americans attend a service of worship in their church. Only a small fraction of that number go to a movie. Yet, when you read this morning's newspaper or watch morning television, there will be no mention of church. Most of the talk is of movies and movie stars, leading one to believe that Hollywood is more important than Jerusalem. In a way, the powers make it so—our lives are in the grip of the images the media offer us. We are incapable, on our own, of thinking about the world other than through the images that the media offer. It takes some superhuman power for us to break free of "the powers."

One of us was talking with a group of students about the alcohol policy on our college campus. "We should be free to drink beer when we want, and how much we want, with no outside coercion from the university administration," said a student. "We should be free to do what we want to do."

Unfortunately, "being free to do what we want to do" is a rather complicated matter. It begs more pressing questions like, "Who are you and what do you want to be when you grow up?" or, "How do you know that what you call 'freedom' only seems free because you lack the imagination to conceive of any kind of life other than the one you are now living?" or, "How do you know what you want to do when you have as yet no goal in mind for where you want to go?"

It was pointed out to the students that beer consumption among American adults has been declining every year in the last two decades—except among one segment of the adult population, young adults about the age of college students. That's why you never see anyone our age in a beer commercial!

And the amazing thing is that, all the time these students are guzzling beer and thinking of themselves as free to do whatever they want, the students are having their strings pulled by Madison Avenue! It is the nature of the powers (like "Wall Street" or "Madison Avenue" or "The Pentagon") to enslave us in the very freedom we thought we were freely enjoying.

In the act of praying this prayer, devils are loosed. The "powers that be" rage against such prayer, can't stand to have one free person running loose who is able to throw off the chains and pray, "Our Father . . . save us."

You know from your own experience that a lie becomes more violent once stripped of its pretense and exposed as a lie. So when you pray to be saved, to be delivered from the test, you are acknowledging that you are not in control of your fate, that there really is something in the world worth resisting, that this world and its rewards are not enough, and that you answer to some greater power than that which the world bows before. Satan masquerades as an angel of light and resists being unmasked. Get ready for a fight.

Note that Paul—*Saint* Paul—wrote these anguished words *after* he had become a Christian:

I do not understand my own actions. For I do not do what I want, but I do the very thing I hate. Now if I do what I do not want, I agree that the law is good. But in fact it is no longer I that do it, but

91

sin that dwells within me. For I know that nothing good dwells within me, that is, in my flesh. I can will what is right, but I cannot do it. For I do not do the good I want, but the evil I do not want is what I do. Now if I do what I do not want, it is no longer I that do it, but sin that dwells within me. . . . Wretched man that I am! Who will rescue me from this body of death? (Romans 7:15-20, 24)

Thus we ask to be rescued in the time of trial, to be delivered from evil. Obviously, something more interesting is going on here than the mere affirmation of a set of beliefs or a search for meaning in life. To be a Christian is not to believe this or that, though certainly we believe in very specific ways, but rather it is to be made part of a people who have learned that they must pray because they are in such fearful struggle. Just by acknowledging Jesus Christ as Lord, in bowing to a ruler other than Caesar, in praising God rather than the American economy for our well-being, we threaten all that is arrayed so fearfully against Christ.

God refused to abandon his conflicted creation. God called forth a new people, by water and the Spirit, Jews and Christians, who are to exemplify for all people what God's providential care of creation looks like. God did not merely create the world, then walk off, leaving us to our own devices. God intruded, continued to create, struggled. We are in a war where God battles the powers of evil. Though we know for sure how the war will end—the cross made clear that God's purposes for creation will not be defeated—there are still battles to be fought.

If God is for us, who is against us? He who did not withhold his own Son, but gave him up for all of us, will he not with him also give us everything else? Who will bring any charge against God's elect? It is God who justifies. Who is to condemn? It is Christ Jesus, who died, yes, who was raised, who is at the right hand of God, who indeed intercedes for us. Who will separate us from the love of Christ? Will hardship, or distress, or persecution, or famine, or nakedness, or peril, or sword? . . . No, in all these things we are more than conquerors through him who loved us. For I am convinced that neither death, nor life, nor angels, nor rulers, nor things present, nor things to come, nor powers . . . will be able to separate us from the love of God in Christ Jesus our Lord.

(Romans 8:31b-39)

We don't know what the future holds, but we do know who holds the future. Knowing that, we have patience in the midst of struggle. Knowing that we live in God's good time, we can take time. The world lives by the story that our lives are rushing toward their conclusion, the oblivion of death and dissolution. We must therefore frantically work to make every minute count—for the world tells us that nothing counts other than what we make. The world attempts to convince us that things are in a terrible mess and it is up to us to set things right or things will never be right. The world tells a story that all suffering, confusion, or pain must be resolved now through earnest human efforts, drugs, economic development, or medical technology, or else life is damned. Violence is the inevitable result of the absence of a story that gives us the freedom to be patient, to take time.

Rejoice in the Lord always; again I will say, Rejoice. Let your gentleness be known to everyone. The Lord is near. Do not worry about anything, but in everything by prayer and supplication with thanksgiving let your requests be made known to God. And the peace of God, which surpasses all understanding, will guard your hearts and your minds in Christ Jesus. (Philippians 4:4-7)

In praying this prayer, we are given something good to do in the meantime. We refuse to let the powers rush us into despair or false hope, premature conclusions or frantic busyness. We are not in a hurry to have things worked out, brought to completion, finished and done because we know that, in Jesus Christ, God has given the world all the time we need.

It takes time and patience, the gradual acquisition of skills to bake bread. And just before this petition, we have prayed for the patience to make daily bread. Resistance to the powers may take the form of marriage, having a family, baking bread—all matters that require communal effort, time, patience, and the acquisition of skills that are not natural and normal. You ought to demand that your church give you the equipment you need to resist the powers.

Because patience is a virtue in short supply in the modern world, because we are enmeshed in the powers, we pray, "Deliver us from evil." Some versions of the Lord's Prayer say "Deliver us from the Evil One." Thus the prayer makes explicit that there is a conspiracy against God's good kingdom in which a personification of evil (Satan) makes sense.

Discipline yourselves, keep alert. Like a roaring lion your adversary the devil prowls around, looking for someone to devour. Resist him, steadfast in your faith. (1 Peter 5:8-9a)

In praying to God to deliver us we acknowledge that God is greater than any foe of God. The power of evil must be admitted and taken seriously, yet not too seriously. Perhaps that is why, though the Lord's Prayer honestly focuses upon trial, temptation and evil, it never mentions Satan by name. Evil is a threatening power, though a defeated one. Though the battle rages, we know who has won the war.

When we pray for deliverance from evil, we acknowledge that we have not the resources, on our own, to resist evil. The Lord's Prayer is so honest. The powers that be are powers over our lives. In our weakness, we reach out and there is deliverance. Isn't that how Alcoholics Anonymous puts it? "We had to reach out to a power greater than ourselves." Note that one of the ways Alcoholics Anonymous enables you to reach out "to a power greater than ourselves" and the chief means through which that power intervenes in our behalf, is by putting you in a group. The community enables us to be free from the powers. Standing alone, as isolated individuals, we are no match for the powers. Therefore we are adopted by a community (church) whereby our prayer "Deliver us from evil" is answered.

Likewise the Spirit helps us in our weakness; for we do not know how to pray as we ought, but that very Spirit intercedes with sighs too deep for words. And God, who searches the heart, knows what is the mind of the Spirit, because the Spirit intercedes for the saints according to the will of God. (Romans 8:26-27)

CHAPTER NINE

"For the kingdom, the power, and the glory are yours now and for ever"

Here comes politics again, one more time as we end our attempt to pray as Jesus taught us. The Lord's Prayer is training in how to understand the political significance of God's Messiah, Jesus. It is a pledge of allegiance to a king and his kingdom that throws all our other allegiances into crisis. Take a trip to Washington, D.C., and you will see this world's kingdom, power, and glory done in marble and granite. There, as in the capital of any nation, the principalities and the powers are given sculptural and architectural embodiment. Everything is bigger than it needs to be, granite, made to appear eternal. Thomas Jefferson is made, in the Jefferson Memorial, to look like a god. Our nations' wars are transformed into crusades. The Declaration of Independence becomes scripture.

The Lord's Prayer has a problem with all that.

We were warned, right at the first, that Jesus was about political disruption, that Jesus was the Messiah, the one who set up a new kingdom and formed a new nation that would resist all the nations and their way of organizing people for good. We were warned by Mary in her "Magnificat," a kind of national anthem for the Jesus movement, that things were going to get rough:

And Mary said,
"My soul magnifies the Lord,
    and my spirit rejoices in God my Savior,
for he has looked with favor on the lowliness of his servant.
    Surely, from now on all generations will call me blessed;
for the Mighty One has done great things for me,
    and holy is his name.
His mercy is for those who fear him
    from generation to generation.
He has shown strength with his arm;
    he has scattered the proud in the thoughts of their hearts.
He has brought down the powerful from their thrones,
    and lifted up the lowly;
he has filled the hungry with good things,
    and sent the rich away empty."

(Luke 1:46-53)

This is salvation, and it is excruciatingly political, economic, and social. When the poor are lifted up and the rich are sent away empty, God's kingdom is breaking out. When the hungry get food, God's kingdom is erupting among us. When a poor, unmarried, pregnant, peasant woman clenches her fist and sings about the victory of God, the folk in the Pentagon, the Kremlin, and Ten Downing Street call out the troops. When a baby cries out in the ghetto and the stars start acting strange, Herod beware. When your congregation prays "Yours is the kingdom, the power, and the glory," the folk at City Hall ought to get nervous. The church exists to sign, to signal, to sing about that tension whereby those who are at the bottom are being lifted up and those who are on top are being sent down.

Stories are told in the Gospels of those who were encountered by the salvation offered in the kingdom, the power, and the glory, yet who went away empty:

A certain ruler asked him, "Good Teacher, what must I do to inherit eternal life?" Jesus said to him, "Why do you call me good? No one is good but God alone. You know the commandments: 'You shall not commit adultery; You shall not murder; You shall not steal; You shall not bear false witness; Honor your father and mother.'" He replied, "I have kept all these since my youth." When Jesus heard this, he said to him, "There is still one thing lacking. Sell all that you own and distribute the money to the poor, and you will have treasure in heaven; then come, follow me." But when he heard this, he became sad; for he was very rich. Jesus looked at him and said, "How hard it is for those who have wealth to enter the kingdom of God! Indeed, it is easier for a camel to go through the eye of a needle than for someone who is rich to enter the kingdom of God."

Those who heard it said, "Then who can be saved?"

(Luke 18:18-26)

The kingdom, the power, and the glory, three large words are piled upon one another here, as the prayer ends, in one final shout of praise to God. Perhaps this prayer ought to be sung, as the church has done in various ways, rather than said. The Lord's Prayer ends in a shout and, as Mary's song reminds us, it makes a great deal of difference how you sing and to whom your songs are addressed. Any army knows the importance of having the right sort of music when marching into battle. Thus we are taught to sing to God, "The kingdom, the power, and the glory are all yours."

Yet do not think that you already know what Christians mean when they use these words. Kingdom, power, and glory are risky, dangerous words. The world loves these words. Kings build their kingdoms and defend them with murderous intensity. Politics is the exercise of power. And glory is what emanates from those who have power. Now, of course, the people are "King"; we live in a democracy. But do not make the mistake of thinking that because democracy has made us kings over ourselves that the church's quarrel with politics has now been resolved. Modern history has demonstrated that democracies are every bit as murderous as dictatorships in defending themselves. The crime rate in the United States suggests that modern democracy, by making each of us kings, gods unto ourselves, has devised a uniquely violent form of government. So we need to take care—when we speak of kingdom, power, and glory—that we unpack these words, that we know what they mean in a peculiar Christian account of what is going on in the world.

Note that in the prayer we speak of kingdom, power, and glory right after we have spoken of temptation and evil. At the very beginning of his ministry, Jesus was led into the wilderness and there Satan offered him all that this world can give:

Then Jesus was led up by the Spirit into the wilderness to be tempted by the devil. He fasted forty days and forty nights, and afterwards he was famished. The tempter came and said to him, "If you are the Son of God, command these stones to become loaves of bread." But he answered, "It is written,
   'One does not live by bread alone,
      but by every word that comes from the mouth of God.'"
Then the devil took him to the holy city and placed him on the pinnacle of the temple, saying to him, "If you are the Son of God, throw yourself down; for it is written,
   'He will command his angels concerning you,'
   and 'On their hands they wil bear you up,
      so that you will not dash your foot against a stone.'"
Jesus said to him, "Again it is written, 'Do not put the Lord your God to the test.'"
   Again, the devil took him to a very high mountain and showed him all the kingdoms of the world and their splendor; and he said to him, "All these I will give you, if you will fall down and worship me." Jesus said to him, "Away with you, Satan! for it is written,

'Worship the Lord your God,
and serve only him.'"
Then the devil left him.

(Matthew 4:1-11a)

Be attentive, in this story of Jesus' temptation, to what Satan offered and what Jesus rejected. Satan offered Jesus only good things—economic power, spiritual power, and political power. Don't we believe in feeding the poor? Don't we gather at church to acquire spiritual proficiency? Don't we believe that Christians ought responsibly to exercise political action for good in our democracy? Jesus rejects them all (even though Satan backs up everything he says with scripture!).

Interestingly, these powers (economic, religious, political) are Satan's to entrust to others as he pleases! Jesus rejects power from Satan's hand. Accepting any of these powers as autonomous, freestanding goods to be exercised by themselves, outside of a relationship to God, make them evil aspects of the worship of Satan. All these goods, which we pervert to evil (many of us are dying from too much bread, religion is a major cause of war, more people have been killed in this century by their own governments than have been killed in war) are transfigured in Christ.

Jesus fed the hungry multitudes (Mark 8:1-10), but as a gift of God's overflowing compassion rather than as an act of economic enslavement. Jesus performed miracles, not as a means of harnessing divine powers for himself, but as sign of God's inbreaking power in the world. Jesus exercised power for good, but not with the means and methods of the world's kingdoms. Unlike our politics, Jesus refused to use violence even for certain good ends. Jesus' life thereby redefined for us the meaning of kingdom, power, and glory.

Let's be honest; we all would love a little glory. We all long for moments when we shine, when we rise above the crowd and radiate success and achievement. Here in the prayer we are giving glory to God, yes. But more than that, praying this prayer rearranges our notions of glory among ourselves.

> *Let the same mind be in you that was in Christ Jesus,*
> *who, though he was in the form of God,*
> *did not regard equality with God*
> *as something to be exploited,*
> *but emptied himself,*
> *taking the form of a slave,*
> *being born in human likeness.*
> *And being found in human form,*
> *he humbled himself*
> *and became obedient to the*
> *point of death—*
> *even death on a cross.*
>
> *Therefore God also highly exalted him*
> *and gave him the name*
> *that is above every name,*
> *so that at the name of Jesus*
> *every name should bend,*
> *in heaven and on earth and under the earth;*
> *and every tongue should confess*
> *that Jesus Christ is Lord,*
> *to the glory of God the Father.*
>
> (Philippians 2:5-11)

In the Gospel of John, Jesus frequently speaks of the "hour of his glory" (John 7:39; 8:54; 12:16, 23; 13:31; 15:8; 21:19). Most misunderstood what Jesus meant by "glory." In John's Gospel, ironically Jesus' "glory" is his cross. As Jesus embraces the cross that the world thrusts upon him, Jesus says:

"Now my soul is troubled. And what should I say—'Father, save me from this hour'? No, it is for this reason that I have come to this hour. Father, glorify your name." Then a voice came from

*heaven, "I have glorified it, and I will glorify it again." The crowd
standing there heard it, and said that it was thunder.*

(John 12:27-29)

Any kingdom that defines glory in terms of a bloody cross
is obviously peculiar. Many people miss the point. From the
beginning, in hearing of the glory of the kingdom, many folk
thought they heard only the sound of thunder. The special
meaning of God's kingdom, power, and glory continues to
be signified to us through the martyrs of the church. The
world deals with threats to its power in the conventional
worldly way—violence. The martyrs responded to the
world's violence in a most unconventional way, by not resisting evil, but by offering their lives as a witness to the
power of God. Not relying on their own power for self-
defense, they put their trust in God. They suffered death,
giving themselves over into the hands of God, trusting the
significance of their lives to God rather than to themselves.
They thus showed their allegiance to a new kingdom, thus
demonstrated a new politics.

In the Middle Ages, the church showed its glorious wisdom by placing statues of the martyrs at the front door, in
the portal of the church. Thus the faithful were welcomed
into the church with scenes of decapitation, bloody swords,
and suffering servants of God. The church, up front, at the
first, portrayed the cost of discipleship.

Though the martyrs may look to the world like powerless
victims, they powerfully unmasked the lies of the world,
powerfully exposed the basis upon which the world's kingdoms prop up themselves. Thus the martyrs point to glory,
but of a new kind. Early Christian art typically portrays the
martyrs with rays of light streaming from their heads. It is a
glorious, stunning thing to see a free woman or man. A
radiance shines from those whose lives are so powerful as to
enable them to stand against the principalities and powers,
to say "No" to the prizes offered in the world's rat race. Thus

the martyrs show us that Jesus not only had the kingdom, the power, and the glory, but he made possible for ordinary women and men like us to participate in the same kingdom, power, and glory. He gave us the means to be saints.

My Father is glorified by this, that you bear much fruit and become my disciples (John 15:8).

One of our favorite hymns speaks of the glory of the saints:

O blest communion, fellowship divine!
We feebly struggle, they in glory shine.
("For All the Saints")

Mother Teresa of Calcutta shines with glory in her work with the dying people of that city. Dorothy Day shone in her rejection of the rewards of this society and in her efforts in behalf of the poor in New York. The world is right to ridicule and to fear such persons for they are a visible, glorious sign of resistance against all that the world worships.

Shortly after speaking explicitly about his crucifixion and the coming hour of his glory, Jesus in John's Gospel speaks of his cross as a political confrontation with the kingdoms of this world:

"Now is the judgment of this world; now the ruler of this world will be driven out. And I, when I am lifted up from the earth, will draw all people to myself." He said this to indicate the kind of death he was to die.
(John 12:31-33)

Finally, the Lord's Prayer says that this kingdom, this power, and this glory, reconceived in life, death, and resurrection of Jesus, is "now and for ever." This kingdom for which we pray is not "pie in the sky by-and-by." The kingdom is now. We must not wait to be friends with God. In Christ, the kingdom of God has been brought near to us.

Usually, the kingdom of God is known now to us only in glimpses. On Sunday, in worship, for instance, there are those wonderful moments when we know the kingdom in its fullness. You come forward for communion, your hands empty, your life empty, and, in blessed bread and wine, you are filled. You stand to pass the peace before coming to the Lord's Table, saying to your sister or brother, "The peace of the Lord," and suddenly this person next to you *is* your relative, family. Peace has been given, not as the world gives.

And yet we pray, "Your kingdom come" and we pray "now and for ever." The kingdom is here, but not yet here in its fullness. The kingdom is now; but also awaited in eternity. Church can be a foretaste of the kingdom of God, but no church is the kingdom of God. Evil is still present, pain is pain, and tragedy is tragedy. God is not finished with us or the world yet. We are on the way, but we have not yet arrived at the end of the journey. By the grace of God, there is more.

We signify this now and not yet quality of the kingdom of God when, in worship, we acclaim "Christ has died, Christ has risen, Christ will come again." We have a story (Christ has died, Christ has risen) that becomes for us the master narrative of what God is doing in the world (Christ will come again). Christ began a journey in which we have been enlisted. We are on the journey and the journey is not yet over. The unfinished aspect of the journey is part of the adventure of discipleship. We keep standing on tiptoes awaiting what God will dare to do among us next.

In the Lord's Supper, we believe that Christ is present, at this table, concretely offering himself to us in bread and wine and communion. In eating this meal together we signify to the world that the world need not wait for the kingdom; the kingdom is being assembled today around the table of the Lord. God's peace is here, so we pass the peace.

Yet we also eat in recognition that the kingdom, the power, and the glory is yet to come in its fullness. We are not satisfied with present arrangements, not at home in this world, not content with what we have. We want more. Our appetite for the living God has been whetted with a bit of bread and a sip of wine and we want more. And, by God's grace, we shall have more. We shall feast at that great banquet open to all ages, nations, and peoples. Christ has died, Christ is risen, Christ will come again.

Then I saw a new heaven and a new earth; for the first heaven and the first earth had passed away, and the sea was no more. And I saw the holy city, the new Jerusalem, coming down out of heaven from God, prepared as a bride adorned for her husband. And I heard a loud voice from the throne saying,

> *"See, the home of God is among mortals.*
> *He will dwell with them as their God;*
> *they will be his peoples,*
> *and God himself will be with them;*
> *he will wipe every tear from their eyes.*
> *Death will be no more;*
> *mourning and crying and pain will be no more,*
> *for the former things have passed away."*
>
> (Revelation 21:1-4)

105

CHAPTER TEN

"Amen"

Sometimes in church, you may hear someone shout, or sometimes mutter, "Amen." It's a Hebrew word meaning "right on," or "so be it." It's a biblical way of saying, "This is *true*." In the Gospels, Jesus frequently says, "Amen, I say to you," usually translated in our English as, "Truly, I say to you."

When we end the prayer with "Amen," it is not only a great moment when the congregation signals its assent to the Lord's Prayer, but it is also a final affirmation that this is true.

All of us long for truth, even though we sometimes live by lies. Here, in the Lord's Prayer, is truth. But we hope that you see truth here, not as a set of propositions to which we assent, a set of beliefs, but rather truth as embodied in Jesus of Nazareth, the one whom we believe to be "the way, and the truth and the life" (John 14:6). He said, "*I* am the way, and the truth, and the life." This truth is a person, personal. We would not know how to pray had not Jesus taught us. Jesus has promised us that we shall be able to worship, "in spirit and truth" (John 4:24). One reason why the Sunday worship of God is not always a pleasant experience is that it is worship in truth.

We would not know truth were it not for being taught this prayer. When people say, "That's true," what they usually mean is that they have some preconception of what truth is and then they affirm whatever assertion matches their preconception. So when they say, "That's true," they mean something like, "That certainly is true to my experience of the world thus far," or "That idea is congruent with all of my previous ideas and is therefore unthreatening to my present existence, therefore it seems true." If they already know the truth as their previous experience or their present existence then they ought to go worship that rather than learn to pray in the Lord's Prayer. For Christians, the Lord's Prayer determines what is true. We wouldn't know truth except through this prayer, which teaches us to whom we belong, where we are moving, what we really look like under our assorted masks, and what true kingdom, power, and glory looks like.

We can't know truth without first being made truthful. We must be transformed, forgiven, born again before we can acknowledge the lies upon which our lives are based, before we can dare to entrust our lives to God to make our lives turn out all right.

I do not cease to give thanks for you as I remember you in my prayers. I pray that the God of our Lord Jesus Christ, the Father of glory, may give you a spirit of wisdom and revelation as you come to know him, so that, with the eyes of your heart enlightened, you may know that is the hope to which he has called you. . . . God put this power to work in Christ when he raised him from the dead and seated him at his right hand in the heavenly places, far above all rule and authority and power and dominion, and above every name that is named, not only in this age but also in the age to come. And he has put all things under his feet and has made him the head over all things for the church, which is his body, the fullness of him who fills all in all. (Ephesians 1:16-18a, 20-23)

One way to become truthful is by praying in public. In public, said aloud, our prayers and our lives are held up to the scrutiny of our sisters and brothers in Christ. We are corrected, held accountable to the witness of the saints. We offer our faith to others and they offer their faith to us and we all are strengthened as disciples in the process. "Private prayer" is a real problem for the church. Our norm is public prayer, prayer in the Sunday assembly, because prayer is about learning how to be truthful and it is virtually impossible to be truthful by yourself.

Devote yourselves to prayer, keeping alert in it with thanksgiving. At the same time pray for us. (Colossians 4:2-3a)

There is something quite helpful in hearing the whole congregation, at the end of the Lord's Prayer, thundering forth with one great "Amen." As we said in the beginning of this book, we pray to *"Our* Father," we ask for forgiveness of *"our* sin," we pray for *"our* daily bread." None of us could make it in this faith alone. We need sisters and brothers in the church, the saints down through the centuries, to teach us to pray. We keep getting it all wrong, praying to the wrong gods, asking for the wrong things. We keep being disappointed when God does not answer our prayer as we thought God ought. We are forever mumbling through the prayer as some disconnected, pious act that we have carefully detached from life. Therefore we desperately need one another. Therefore we can't pray as Jesus taught us without the church. Amen.

In a prison camp in World War II, on a cold, dark evening after a series of beatings, after the hundreds of prisoners of war had been marched before the camp commander and harangued for an hour, when the prisoners were returned to their dark barracks and told to be quiet for the rest of the night, someone, somewhere in one of the barracks began saying the Lord's Prayer. Some of his fellow prisoners lying next to him began to pray with him. Their prayer was overheard by prisoners in the next building who joined them. One by one, each set of barracks joined in the prayer until, as the prayer was ending with, "Thine is the kingdom, the power, and the glory," hundreds of prisoners had joined their voices in a strong, growing, defiant prayer, reaching a thunderous, "Amen!"

And then the camp was silent, but not before the tables had been turned, the prisoners had thrown off their chains, and a new world had been sighted, signaled, and stated.

Wherever, since the day that Jesus taught us, this prayer has been prayed, even in the darkest of days, the worst of situations, prisoners have been set free, the blind see, the lame walk, the poor have good news proclaimed to them, and a new world, not otherwise available to us, has been constituted.

As the great theologian Karl Barth said, "To clasp hands in prayer is the beginning of an uprising against the disorder of the world."

One of the others in the group was heard to say, "I'm not so sure. Praying that prayer on the steps of the courthouse certainly changed me. And that's a start." Amen.

One of us remembers worshiping in a predominantly African American congregation were the "Amens" were frequent and outspoken during the entire service, but especially during the sermon. When, during the sermon that day, the preacher said something about, "Each of us had better use this time to tell the Lord what we haven't had the heart to tell him all this week!" The preacher's words sailed past us until a fellow worshiper, a woman seated in the pew just behind us yelled, "Amen! Tell it Preacher!"

Her "Amen!" reminded us that we had better listen to the preacher, that the words which so unthreateningly bounced off of us were words meant by God for us. The words were not only wise; they were true. They were not only true; they were true for me. Amen.

Another image. One of us was visiting his mother in a nursing home. One of the things we all fear today is nursing homes. A Sunday service was being held in the cafeteria, the kind of setting we all fear. The congregation was composed of elderly people, most of whom appeared to be unaware of where they were. The preacher preached enthusiastically. The preacher sang enthusiastically. There was no response from the congregation.

Then the minister said, "Let us pray. Our Father...." Suddenly, everyone joined in. There was a congregation. Their bodies remembered the prayer. What better way to have our lives end than to be embodied in this prayer? Finally, this is what this book has been about. This is what it means to have the gift of this prayer. Amen.

In teaching us to pray, Jesus is making us more truthful, more faithful. Jesus is making us his disciples. In praying, our lives are being bent away from their natural inclinations toward God. We are becoming the very holiness, obedience, forgiveness for which we ask for in the prayer. Prayed in its usual place in the liturgy, toward the end of Sunday worship, after the Prayer of Thanksgiving, aloud, as one great, doxological shout of praise, the Lord's Prayer becomes the summary, the crescendo of the church's worship. We find our little lives caught up in the great drama of God's redemption of the world, we are swept up into an adventure more significant than our lives would have been if left to ourselves, heaven is open, the kingdom is come, and we shout, "Amen!"

I thank my God every time I remember you, constantly praying with joy in every one of my prayers for all of you . . . I am confident of this, that the one who began a good work among you will bring it to completion by the day of Jesus Christ. (Philippians 1:3-4, 6)

Let the last words of the New Testament serve as our last word, our Amen:

> *"Surely I am coming soon."*
> *Amen. Come, Lord Jesus!*
> *The grace of the Lord Jesus be with all the saints. Amen.*
> (Revelation 22:20-21)

110

Scripture Index

111

Name Index

49295521R00064

Made in the USA
Lexington, KY
31 January 2016